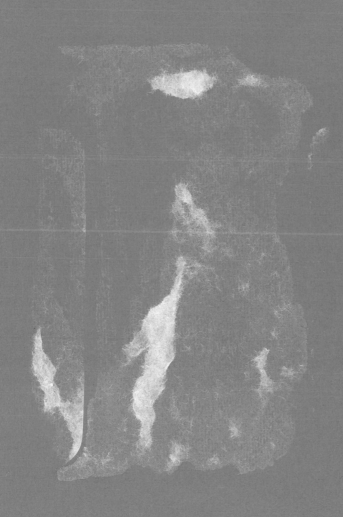

The Literature of Cinema

ADVISORY EDITOR: **MARTIN S. DWORKIN**
INSTITUTE OF PHILOSOPHY AND POLITICS OF EDUCATION
TEACHER'S COLLEGE, COLUMBIA UNIVERSITY

THE LITERATURE OF CINEMA presents a comprehensive selection from the multitude of writings about cinema, rediscovering materials on its origins, history, theoretical principles and techniques, aesthetics, economics, and effects on societies and individuals. Included are works of inherent, lasting merit and others of primarily historical significance. These provide essential resources for serious study and critical enjoyment of the "magic shadows" that became one of the decisive cultural forces of modern times.

Screen Monographs I

THE ART OF CINEPLASTICS
Elie Faure

THE TECHNIQUE OF THE FILM
Bernard Gordon and Julian Zimet

PARNASSUS TO LET
Eric Walter White

ARNO PRESS & THE NEW YORK TIMES

New York • 1970

Reprint Edition 1970 by Arno Press Inc.
Reprinted from copies in The Museum of Modern Art Library
and The Library of Congress
Library of Congress Catalog Card Number: 75-124020
ISBN 0-405-01626-3
ISBN for complete set: 0-405-01600-X
Manufactured in the United States of America

The Art of
Cineplastics

BY

ELIE FAURE

Translated from the French by
WALTER PACH

BOSTON
THE FOUR SEAS COMPANY
1923

The Four Seas Press
Boston, Mass., U.S.A.

These essays originally appeared in English in the pages of "The Freeman" (New York) and are here reprinted through the courtesy of its editors.

The Art of Cineplastics

The Art of Cineplastics

I

I AM regarded, in my own circle, as one who hates the theatre. On this point, I am even accused of bearing the stigmata of religion, of expressing some obscure atavistic protest as of one whose ancestors have always gone to the confessional and who therefore is opposed to the exaggerated modern taste for a spectacle that is said to be immoral. Perhaps there is something in this. When I question myself, however, I am unable to see, in this aspect of my "hatred" for the theatre, any other than a remote point of departure. All our opinions originate in feelings which we generally get from our immediate education or from a reaction against it—and beyond which we do not go if we have not learned to think. The urge towards thought leads us, however, sooner or later, either radically to modify our first feeling or else—and more frequently it seems to me—to seek and find, by analysis, the justification of the feeling. It is a means of

9

keeping intact that inner pride which constitutes our spiritual skeleton and defines our personality.

It is thus that I have been able to arrive at an explanation—acceptable to myself—of my "hatred" of the theatre. It is true that I do not care for the theatre so much that I never miss a new play, or return to one seven times over. I like it, if I may say so, in the same way that I like painting, in a way of my own, which puts me under no obligation to visit every exhibition, or to swallow all the dust and stupidities one gets there from four to six in the afternoon. That may mean, perhaps it ought to mean, that I do not care for pictures. Yet I like Veronese, Rembrandt, Goya, Cézanne, and some others; and if I carry my contempt for literature to such a point that it never occurs to me to subscribe to one of those libraries that provide you, perhaps, with all the novels of the week, I like Montaigne, Pascal, Baudelaire, Stendhal. Thus, having admitted that I really have a "hatred" of the theatre, I will confess tht I love Racine, Molière, and Shakespeare, and that it seems to me that the Greek tragedians realized, in their day, something very great indeed.

The love of the theatre for the sake of the
theatre has led our generation to a curious intellectual and sentimental deformation. It draws
from the theatre a sort of factitious excitement,
quite analogous to that which is obained through
morphine, alcohol or tobacco—an imperious, irresistible, almost painful need to return at short
intervals and acclaim as a masterpiece the drug
that is served there; for the stimulation it gives
its devotees really provides them with the cour-
age to wait two, three or six days before asking
from a similar drug, taken in always stronger
doses, a new and always more necessary stimulation. It seems certain to me that the morbid
unanimity with which people love the theatre
indicates both the decomposition of society and
the decomposition of the theatre. In saying this
let it be remembered that I am making a statement, not indulging in recriminations. All the
arts die from the generalizing of the taste that
leads to them—from the generalizing of the
talents which permit them to maintain that taste,
refine it, and at last render it banal; thus painting
and the novel in other periods, and doubtless

again to-morrow; the theatre to-day. The fact
that there exist thirty or forty dramatic authors
enjoying a world-wide reputation, a literary glory
meriting all the official honors, is typical, as is the
fact that the actor has assumed, in our day, the
fabulous importance, comic or terrible, as the
case may be, which we know.

Rousseau, who was a very great artist, but who
always used to choose moral pretexts for the
rebuilding of his faith, was only too right, more
than a hundred and fifty years ago, when he
considered the theatre as an organ of moral dissolution. Would he not perceive in our day, when
the theatre has grown a hundredfold in importance without any increase in theatrical genius—
although theatrical talents have mutiplied sick-
eningly—would he not perceive that the social
dissolution indicated by the theatre of to-day is
taking on a character twice as general, twice as
important and, I would add, twice as consoling
as regards the immediate morrow, as the one
with which he reproached the theatre of all time?
Every great collective—or if it be preferred,
social—spectacle, preserved in the unity and

majesty of its power—the Greek drama, for example—imprints on an entire people an æsthetic discipline which, in the time of Rousseau, thanks to the classic age before him, still retained some vigour, a vigour that Voltaire destroyed. The nineteenth century, with its immense productivity, killed the theatre and showed itself, appearances notwithstanding, equally ill-adapted for the collective or social art *par excellence,* namely: architecture. Let anyone name for me, in France, one play—literally *one* play—which, since the death of Racine, may be considered a masterpiece of the theatre—something, that is, possessing a collective dramatic architecture such as will raise an entire crowd to the height of a unanimous, firmly constructed, stylicized conception of fate and the world. "Turcaret" is nothing more than a painting of character which might have been undertaken with equal success in a novel. The plays of Beaumarchais or Mirbeau belong to political satire or even polemics.

II

So it is; in the end my "hatred" of the theatre leads me to a statement that could hardly have been expected of me. I consider it, in its essence, as one of the highest of the arts, if not the highest of all. It has, in this essence, the great character of great art, a sort of impersonality, the fierce nakedness of a construction made to be seen by all, and by all at the same time, and wherein all may find, summed up, abridged by its passage through the spirit, the monumental import which they recognize, or which their fathers recognized, in their religion, for example; something that defines them to themselves, that is like a majestic bridge springing at one end from their feelings, their passions, their education, and their customs, and at the other from their need for eternity and the absolute they wish to attain in it. The comic, the tragic—it matters not at all. Æschylus, Aristophanes, Shakespeare, and Molière are brothers. At the base of all their arts, an immense pessimistic sentiment regarding the world manifests itself by a victorious returning

upon itself of the will—in a triumphant laugh
or a proud fronting of the cruelty of the gods.

As far back as we look, among all the peoples
of the earth, and at all times, a collective spectacle
has alone been able to unite all classes, all ages,
and, as a rule, the two sexes, in a unanimous
communion exalting the rhythmic power that
defines, in each one of them, the moral order.
Whatever the collective spectacle may be, although it does not necessarily have the same
character at all times (in fact it rarely has quite
the same character), it possesses one consistent
property everywhere: every one assists at it, side
by side, in a given spot, in a building or in the
open air, covered or open to the sky, in circles
or semi-circles raised one above another so that
all may see from their places, whatever their
social rank or their fortune may be.

Here already is a point where the theatre of
to-day seems to me to have degenerated. The
spectacle has almost always and almost everywhere assumed a plastic character, even among
the Jews, the least plastic people on earth, who
had their religious dances and whose most thrilling memory is that of their first king dancing

before their first mystic symbol. Perhaps an exception is to be made in the case of the Germans, with whom symphonic music replaces by an audition in common, the seeing in common that is necessary to all groups of men. We find the dance among all the peoples of the Orient, the Mesopotamians, the Egyptians and the Arabs, among whom the narrative, amid a circle of auditors, takes on the national and even sacred character of an invincible custom that engenders interminable cycles of legends—always returning, for the communion of laughter or of tears, to the same circle, where the same story-teller mimics, drones, and sings, just as he has been doing for these thousands of years.

Thus we have the games of the stadium, and notably the religious drama of the Hellenes, wherein the music, the dancing, and the psychological development of the tragedy of passion finally culminate in certain aggrandized, stylicized, unchangeable forms, evolving on the stage and realizing a momentary equilibrium between a sensual orgy and the discipline of the spirit. Thus, among the most positive, the least visionary people on the earth, we have chariot-races, pitched battlès, contests in the centre of a stone circus holding eighty thousand spectators. Thus we have the chanted and acted mystery, framed in the ritual gestures of a procession and a mass, in the cathedral of the Christians; the voice of the plain-song, the ribbing of stone, and the color of the stained glass enveloping the actors and the spectators in a common, supernatural atmosphere that gives to the mystic interchange a character of absoluteness. Thus we have the theatrical unity and the regulated ballet of the people of the Renaissance with their classical feeling which, with the analysis of the philosophers, and with individualism in acting, degenerates so quickly till it loses all collective significance and the art is drowned in the erotic and bestial frenzy of the plays of the modern drawing-rooms and public dance-halls.

Dramatic style has been lost. The individual flounders about alone, which is the very negation of the art which this individual, gifted as he may be, genius that he may be, attempts alone to represent. The drama has become a means of enriching the author, who sets himself the servile task of discovering and flattering the latest sentimental impulses, the latest weekly fashions of a public that is no longer stirred by any great common feeling; it is a means of pushing forward the actor for whom the play is written and who subordinates it, on the one hand, to the manias of his spectators and, on the other, to his own success. Even when he is interesting and personal, the actor effaces his associates; the play exists only to attest in a violent sort of way the mannerisms and stage-tricks, the comic or dramatic qualities that are his specialty, leaving the rest of the company in a sort of dubious shadow and reducing the work itself to the rôle of one of those concertos which dishonor the art of music in order to permit certain ephebes with long, oily hair to execute their acrobatics on the piano or the violin; how cruelly one suffers during their torturing performances, how eagerly one wants to cry out, "Enough!"

Between the actor and the author, between the actor and the public, there are the same charming relationships that bind the successful office-seeker to his party, the elected to the elector. So it is that the theatre and politics constitute very analogous spectacles, frequented by the same enthusiasts as the law-courts. The whole dramatic art[1] has taken refuge in the clown, the sole survivor of the plastic epic of the theatre —isolated thus, and rendered almost terrible because of it; for the clown imagines, composes and acts his part, which is self-sufficing and makes a unity, like a picture, a sonata, a poem, in which no intermediary comes between the public and the art, which imposes on the public its own power of conception and its own faculty for creation.

III

WITH dramatic style lost, the present is-just the moment for the theatre to choose for its attempt to monopolize an art, or at least the instrument of an art, that is absolutely new; one that is so rich in resources that, after having transformed the spectacle, it can act on the æsthetic and social transformation of man himself with a power which I consider to exceed the most extravagant

[1] The attempt Copeau is making is only a phenomenon, an exception which proves the rule and shows in a more cruel light, by contrast, the degeneracy of the theatre.

predictions made for it.[1] I·see such power in the
art of the moving picture that I do not hesitate
to regard it as the nucleus of the common spectacle which every one demands, as being perfectly susceptible of assuming a grave, splendid,
moving character, a religious character even, in
the universal, majestic sense of the word. It can
do so quite as well as music, which began with
some sort of string stretched between two sticks,
struck by the finger of some poor devil, black or

[1] Since this essay was written, the cinegraphic
production of the world does not seem to have
improved. The cinema, which was severely injured
by the novel of episode, has turned to the even more
wretched melodrama. I still believe in it, but it is,
like the other arts, a victim of the political and
social chaos in which the whole world is floundering.
Is it destined, as I would still like to think, in a
rejuvenated society, to become the art of the mass,
the centre of a powerful communion in which new
symphonic forms will be born in the tumult of passion and used with aesthetic ends capable of lifting
the heart? Is it destined, if the customs of demo-
cratic society persist, to specialize like other forms
of art, to furnish sentimental insanities for the
appetite of the mob, is it destined to yield its hidden
harmonies only to the initiate? I hope not. Like the
other arts it needs for its regeneration—and, in its
own particular case, since it is at the beginning of
its career, even to attain its first really aesthetic
phase—to be steeped completely in the needs of the
people, to be a prey to some quickening illusion.

yellow, blind perhaps, to an even and monotonous rhythm; it can do so quite as well as the dance, which began with some little girl skipping from one foot to the other, while around her other children clapped their hands; quite as well as the theatre, which began with the mimicking recital of some adventure of war or the chase amid a circle of auditors; quite as well as architecture, which began with the arranging of a cave, in front of which, after a fire had been lighted, some one stretched the hide of an aurochs; quite as well as the frescoes, the statues, and the perspectives of the temple, which began with the silhouette of a horse or a deer, dug out with a flint on a bit of bone or ivory.

The needs and desires of man, fortunately, are stronger than his habits. There will some day be an end of the cinema considered as an off-shoot of the theatre, an end of the sentimental monkey-tricks and gesticulations of gentlemen with blue chins and rickety legs, made up as Neapolitan boatmen or Icelandic fishermen; and ladies really too mature for *ingénue* parts who, with their eyes turned heavenward and their hands clasped, ask the benediction of heaven and

the protection of the crowd for the orphan perse-
cuted by the wicked rich man. It is impossible
that these things should not disappear along with
the theatre of which they are the counterpart.
Otherwise, we must look to America and Asia,
the new peoples or those renewed by death, to
bring in—with the fresh air of the oceans and
the prairies—brutality, health, youth, danger, and
freedom of action.

The cinema has nothing in common with the
theatre save this, which is only a matter of
appearances, and the most external and banal
appearances at that: it is, as the theatre is, but
also as are the dance, the games of the stadium
and the procession, a collective spectacle having
as its intermediary an actor. It is even less near
to the theatre than to the dance, the games or the
procession, in which I see only one kind of intermediary between the author and the public.
Actually the cinema presents, between the author
and the public, three intermediaries, the actor—
let us call him the cinemimic,—the camera, and
the photographer. (I do not speak of the screen,
which is a material accessory, forming a part of
the hall, like the setting in the theatre.) This

already establishes the cinema as farther away
from the theatre than from music, in which there
also exist two intermediaries between the composer and the public—i.e., the player and the
instrument. Finally, and especially, there is no
speaking in the cinema, which is certainly not an
essential characteristic of the theatre. Charlot
(Charlie Chaplin), the greatest of cinemimics,
never opens his mouth; and observe that the best
films almost completely do without those intolerable explanations of which the screen is so
prodigal.

In the cinema the whole drama unrolls in absolute silence, from which not only words, but the
noise of feet, the sound of the wind and the
crowds, all the murmurs, all the tones of nature
are absent. The pantomime? The relationship is
scarcely closer there. In the pantomime, as in the
theatre, the composition and the realization of the
rôle change, more or less, every evening, which
confers on both a sentimental, even impulsive
character. The composition of the film, on the
other hand, is fixed once for all, and once fixed it
does not change again, which gives it a character
that the plastic arts are the only ones to possess.

Besides, pantomime represents, by stylicized gestures, the feeling and the passions brought to their essential attitudes: it is a psychological art before being a plastic art. The cinema is plastic first: is represents a sort of moving architecture which is in constant accord, in a state of equilibrium dynamically pursued—with the surroundings and the landscapes where it is erected and falls to the earth again. The feelings and the passions are hardly more than a pretext, serving to give a certain sequence, a certain probability to the action.

Let us not misunderstand the meaning of the word "plastic." Too often it evokes the motionless, colorless forms called sculptural—which lead all too quickly to the academic canon, to helmeted heroism, to allegories in sugar, zinc, papier mâché or lard. Plastics is the art of expressing form in repose or in movement by all the means that man commands: full-round, bas-relief, engraving on the wall, or on copper, wood or stone, drawing in any medium, painting, fresco, the dance; and it seems to me in no wise over-bold to affirm that the rhythmic movements of a group of gymnasts or of a processional or military column touch the spirit of plastic art far more nearly than do the pictures of the school of David. Like painting, moreover—and more completely than painting, since a living rhythm and its repetition in time are what characterize cineplastics—the later art tends and will tend more every day to approach music and the dance as well. The interpenetration, the crossing and the association of movements and cadences already give us the impression that even the most mediocre films unroll in musical space.

I remember the unexpected emotions I received, seven or eight years before the war, from certain films the scenarios of which, as it happens, were of an incredible silliness. The revelation of what the cinema of the future can be came to me one day; I retain an exact memory of it, of the commotion that I experienced when I observed, in a flash, the magnificence there was in the relationship of a piece of black clothing to the grey wall of an inn. From that moment I paid no more attention to the martyrdom of the poor woman who was condemned, in order to save her husband from dishonor, to give herself to the lascivious banker who had previously mur-

dered her mother and debauched her child. I
discovered, with increasing astonishment, that,
thanks to the tone-relations that were transform-
ing the film for me in a system of colors scaling
from white to black and ceaselessly commingled,
moving, changing on the surface and in the depth
of the screen, I was witnessing a sudden coming
to life, a descent into that host of personages
whom I had already seen—motionless—on the
canvases of Greco, Frans Hals, Rembrandt,
Velazquez, Vermeer, Courbet, Manet.[1] I do not
set down these names at random, the last two
especially. They are those the cinema suggested
to me from the first.

Later, as the medium of the screen was per-
fected from day to day, as my eye became accustomed to these strange works, other memories
associated themselves with the earlier ones, till
I no longer needed to appeal to my memory and
invoke familiar paintings in order to justify the

[1] May I be permitted in passing to form a wish?
It is that smoking be forbidden in cinema halls, as
talking is forbidden in concert halls. At the end of
an hour the atmosphere is saturated with smoke.
The finest films are clouded, lose their transparency
and their quality, both in tone and overtone.

new plastic impressions that I got at the cinema.
Their elements, their complexity which varies
and winds in a continuous movement, the constantly unexpected things imposed on the work
by its mobile composition, ceaselessly renewed,
ceaselessly broken and remade, fading away and
reviving and breaking down, monumental for one
flashing instant, impressionistic the second following—all this constitutes a phenomenon too
radically new for us even to dream of classing it
with painting, or with sculpture, or with the
dance, least of all with the modern theatre. It is
an unknown art that is beginning, one that to-day
is as far perhaps from what it will be a century
hence, as the Negro orchestra, composed of a
tom-tom, a bugle, a string across a calabash, and
a whistle, is from a symphony composed and
conducted by Beethoven.

I would point out the immense resources which,
independent of the acting of the cinemimics, are
beginning to be drawn from their multiple and
incessantly modified relationships with the surroundings, the landscape, the calm, the fury, and
the caprice of the elements, from natural or artificial lighting, from the prodigiously complex and

shaded play of values, from precipitate or retarded movements, such as the slow movements of those galloping horses which seem to be made of living bronze, of those running dogs whose muscular contractions recall the undulations of reptiles. I would point out, too, the profound universe of the microscopic infinite, and perhaps —tomorrow—of the telescopic infinite, the un-dreamed-of dance of atoms and stars, the shadows under the sea as they begin to be shot with light. I would point out the majestic unity of masses in movement that all this accentuates without insistence, as if it were playing with the grandiose problem that Masaccio, Leonardo, Rembrandt were never quite able to solve . . . I could never come to the end of it. Shakespeare was once a formless embryo in the narrow shadows of the womb of a good dame of Stratford.

IV

THAT the starting-point of the art of the moving picture is in plastics, seems to be beyond all doubt. To whatever form of expression, as yet scarcely suspected, it may lead us, it is by volumes, arabesques, gestures, attitudes, relationships, associations, contrasts and passages of tones—the whole animated and insensibly modified from one fraction of a second to another—that it will impress our sensibility and act on our intelligence by the intermediation of our eyes. Art, I have called it, not science. It is doubly, even trebly art, for there is conception, composition, creation, and transcription to the screen on the part of three persons, the author, the producer, the photographer, and of a group of persons, the cinemimics, as the actors may properly be called. It would be desirable, and possible, for the author to make his own film-pictures, and better still if one of the cinemimics, since he can not be his own photographer, were to be the composer and producer of the work to which he gives life and often transfigures by his genius. This is, of course, just what certain American cinemimics are doing, notably the admirable Charlie Chaplin. It is a moot question whether the author of the cinematographic scenario—I hesitate to create the word cineplast—should be a writer or a painter, whether the cinemimic should be a mimic or an actor. Charlie Chaplin solves all these questions; a new art presupposes a new artist.

A certain literary critic has recently deplored the sacrificing of the theatre to the cinema and has bracketed Charlie Chaplin and Rigadin (an actor who was formerly known in the French theatre under the name of Dranem) in the same terms of reprobation. This does not mean at all that the the critic in question is unequal to his task when he sticks to the field of literature; it means simply that he does not realize the artistic significance of the cinema, nor the difference of quality that necessarily exists between the cinema and the theatre and between one film and another. For, with all due respect to this critic, there is a greater distance between Charlie Chaplin and Rigadin than between William Shakespeare and Edmond Rostand. I do not write the name of Shakespeare at random. It answers perfectly to the impression of divine intoxication that Charlie

Chaplin gives me, for example, in his film, "An Idyll of the Fields"; it befits that marvelous art of his, with its mingling of deep melancholy and fantasy, an art that races, increases, decreases and then starts off like a flame again, carrying to each sinuous mountain-ridge over which it winds the very essence of the spiritual life of the world, that mysterious light through which we half perceive that our laughter is a triumph over our pitiless insight, that our joy is the feeling of a sure eternity imposed by ourselves upon nothingness, that an elf, a goblin, a gnome dancing in a landscape of Corot, into which the privilege of reverie precipitates him who suffers, bears God himself in his heart.

We must, I think, take our stand on this. Chaplin comes from America, he is the authentic genius of a school that is looming up more and more as the first in importance in cineplastics. I have heard that the Americans greatly enjoy our French films, with their representation of French customs—a fine thing, to be sure, but without the least relation to the effects of motion which are the essential foundation of cinematographic art. The French film, as we know it,

is resolutely idealistic. It stands for something
like the painting of Ary Scheffer at the time
when Delacroix was strugggling.[1] The French
film is only a bastard form of a degenerate
theatre, and seems for that reason to be destined
to poverty and death if it does not take a new
turn.

The American film, on the other hand, is a
new art, full of immense perspectives, full of the
promise of a great future. I imagine that the
taste of the Americans for the "damaged goods"
that we export to them is to be explained by the
well-known attraction that forms of art in a
state of decomposition exercise on all primitive
peoples. For the Americans are primitive and at
the same time barbarous, which accounts for the
strength and vitality which they infuse into the
cinema. It is among them that the cinema will,
I believe, assume its full significance as plastic
drama in action, occupying time through its own
movement and carrying with it its own space, of

[1] There were in France at the time these lines
were written and there have been since, interesting
efforts in the direction of the true cinema. In particular, those of Monsieur Marcel L'Herbier, Monsieur
H. Krauss, Monsieur Delluc.

a kind that places it, balances it, and gives it the
social and psychological value it has for us. It
is natural that when a new art appears in the
world it should choose a new people which has
had hitherto .no really personal art. Especially
when this new art is bound up, through the
medium of human gesture, with the power, defi-
niteness and firmness of action. Especially, too,
when this new people is accustomed to introduce
into every department of life an increasingly
complicated mechanical system, one that more
and more hastens to produce, associate and precipitate movements; and especially when this art
can not exist without the most accurate scientific
apparatus of a kind that has behind it no tradi-
tions, and is organized, as it were, physiologically,
with the race that employs it.

Cineplastics, in fact, presents a curious characteristic which music alone, to a far less marked
degree, has exhibited hitherto. In cineplastics it
is far from being true, as it is in the case of the
other arts, that the feeling of the artist creates
the art; in cineplastics it is the art that is creating
its artists. We know that the great thing we call
the symphony was engendered little by little by

the number and the increasing complexity of
musical instruments; but before even the instrument with one string, man already sang, clapping
his hands and stamping his feet: here we had a
science first, and nothing but a science. There
was required the grandiose imagination of man
to introduce into it, at first by a timid infiltration,
and later by a progressive invasion breaking
down all barriers, his power of organizing facts
according to his own ideas, so that the scattered
objects that surround him are transformed into
a coherent edifice, wherein he seeks the fecund
and always renewed illusion that his destiny de-
velops in conformity with his will.

Hence come these new plastic poems which
transport us in three seconds from the wooded
banks of a river that elephants cross, leaving a
long track of foam, to the heart of wild mountains where distant horsemen pursue one another
through the smoke of their rifle-shots, and from
evil taverns where powerful shadows bend over
a death-bed in mysterious lights, to the weird
half-light of submarine waters where fish wind
through grottos of coral. Indeed—and this
comes at unexpected moments, and in comic films

as well as in the others—animals may take part
in these dramas and new-born children, too, and
they participate by their play, their joys, their
disappointments, their obscure dramas of instinct,
all of which the theatre, as it seems to me, is
quite incapable of showing us. Landscapes, too,
beautiful or tragic or marvellous, enter the moving symphony in order to add to its human meaning, or to introduce into it, after the fashion of
a stormy sky by Delacroix or a silver sea by
Veronese, the sense of the supernatural.

I have already explained why the Americans
have understood, as by instinct, the direction they
should give to their visual imagination, letting
themselves be guided by their love for space,
movement and action. As for the Italians they
might be reborn to the life of conquest and lose
the memory of their classic works, were they
to find in their genius for gesture and attitude
and for setting (thanks in part to the aid of their
wonderful sunshine, which is like the sunshine
of California) the elements of another original
school, less violent and also less sober, but presenting better qualities of composition than that
of the Americans. In the cinema the Italians

give us marvellously the crowd, and the historical
drama in the motionless setting of palaces, gar-
dens, ruins, where the ardent life that character-
izes the Italian people goes on, with that quality
which is theirs of never appearing out of time
or out of place. A gesticulating drama it may be,
but the gestures are true. The Italian gesture
has been called theatrical; but it is not that, for
it is sincere. Giotto's personages are not acting.
If that is the impression we get from Bolognese
painting, it is because the Bolognese no longer
represented the real genius of Italy. Rembrandt,
up to the age of forty-five, and Rubens, are far
more theatrical than all the Italian masters down
to the painters of Bologna. Italian energy alone
will render the Italian school of cineplastics
capable of maintaining in this new art in which
the Americans already excel, the plastic genius
of Europe, and that by creating a form that is
destined to have a great future.[1]

In any case, the chief triumph in the American
conception of cineplastics—a triumph which the

[1] For the last two years the Italian film seems to
be in decay. On the contrary, Doctor Caligari has
recently revealed the powerful inventive genius of
the German film.

Italians approach most nearly and the French
approach, alas, most remotely—seems to me to
consist in this: that the subject is nothing but a
pretext. The web of feeling should be nothing
but the skeleton of the autonomous organism
represented by the film. In time this web must
be woven into the plastic drama. It is evident
that this drama will be the more moving in pro-
portion as the moral and psychological pattern
that it covers is strongly, soberly, and logically
conducted. But that is all. The expression and
the effects of that drama remain in the domain
of plastics; and the web of feeling is there only
to reveal and increase their value.

V

SHALL I dare to dream of a future for the art of
the moving picture, a future distant no doubt,
when the actor, or as I would prefer to call him,
the cinemimic, shall disappear or at least be
specialized, and when the cineplast shall dominate
the drama of form that is precipitated in time?
Observe, in the first place, one vital point that

hitherto has not been sufficiently noted, I think, or at least the poetic consequences of which have not been made sufficiently clear. The cinema incorporates time in space. More than this, through the cinema, time really becomes a dimension of space. We shall be able to see dust rising, spreading, dissipating, a thousand years after it has spurted up from the road under the hoofs of a horse; we shall be able to see for a thousand years the smoke of a cigarette condensing and then entering the ether—and this in a frame of space under our very eyes. We shall be able to understand how it may be that the inhabitants of a distant star, if they can see things on earth with powerful telescopes, are really contemporaries of Jesus, since at the moment when I write these lines they may be witnessing his crucifixion, and perhaps making a photographic or even cinematographic record of the scene, for we know that the light that illumines us takes nineteen or twenty centuries to reach them. We can even imagine, and this may modify still more our idea of the duration of time, that we may one day see this film, taken on that distant star, either through the inhabitants

sending it to us in some sort of projectile or perhaps transmitting it to our screens by some system of interplanetary projection. This, which is
not scientifically impossible, would actually make
us the contemporaries of events which had taken
place a hundred centuries before us, and in the
very place wherein we live.

In the cinema we have indeed already made
of time an instrument that plays its rôle in the
whole spatial organism, unfurling under our eyes
its successive masses which are ceaselessly
brought before us in dimensions that permit us
to grasp their extent in surface-area and in depth.
Already we find in these masses pleasures of an
intensity unknown hitherto. Stop the most beautiful film you know, make of it at any moment
an inert photograph, and you will not obtain even
a memory of the emotion that it gave you as a
moving picture.

Thus in the cinema time clearly becomes
necessary for us. Increasingly it forms a part of
the always more dynamic idea that we are receiv-
ing about the object upon which we are gazing.
We play with it at our ease. We can speed it
up. We can slow it down. We can suppress

it. Indeed I feel it as being formerly part
of myself, as enclosed alive, with the very
space which it measures and which measures it,
within the walls of my brain. Homer becomes
my contemporary, as my lamp upon my table
before me is my contemporary, since Homer had
his share in the elaboration of the image under
which my lamp appears to me. Since the idea
of duration enters the idea of space as a constitu-
ent element, we may easily imagine an expanded
cineplastic art which shall be no more than an
architecture of the idea, and from which the
cinemimic will, as I have said, disappear, because
only a great artist will be able to build edifices
that are made and broken down and remade
ceaselessly—by imperceptible passages of tone
and modelling that are in themselves architecture
at every moment—without our being able to seize
the thousandth part of a second in which the
transition takes place.

I remember witnessing something analogous
to this in nature itself. At Naples, in 1906, I
saw the great eruption of Vesuvius. The plume
of smoke, two thousand metres high, that rose
above the mouth of the volcano was spherical,

outlined against the sky and sharply separated from it. Inside this cloud, enormous masses of ashes assumed form and became formless unceasingly, all sharing in the modelling of the great sphere and producing an undulation on its surface, moving and varying, but sustained, as if by an attraction at the centre, in the general mass, the form and dimensions of which nothing appeared to alter. In a flash it seemed to me as I looked upon the phenomenon that I had grasped the law of the birth of planets, held by gravitation around the solar nucleus. It seemed to me that I was looking at a symbolic form of that grandiose art of which in the cinema we now perceive the germ, the development of which the future doubtless holds in store for us, namely: a great moving construction ceaselessly reborn of itself under our eyes by virtue of its inner forces alone. Human, animal, vegetable, and inert forms, in all their immense variety, have their share in the building of it, whether a multitude is employed on the work or whether only one man is able to realize it in its totality.

Perhaps I may explain myself further on this last point. We all know those animated draw-

ings, very dry and thin and stiff, which are sometimes projected on the screen and are, when compared with the forms that I have been imagining,
what the outlines in chalk traced on a blackboard
by a child are to the frescoes of Tintoretto and
the canvases of Rembrandt. Now let us suppose
three or four generations devoted to the problem
of giving depth to these images, not by surfaces
and lines but by thickness and volumes; three or
four generations devoted to modelling, by values
and half-tones, a series of successive movements
which after a long training would gradually enter
into our habits, even into our unconscious actions,
till the artist was enabled to use them at will, for
drama or idyll, comedy or epic, in the light or
in the shadow, in the forest, the city, or the
desert. Suppose that an artist thus armed has
the heart of a Delacroix, the power of realization
of a Rubens, the passion of a Goya, and the
strength of a Michelangelo: he will throw on the
screen a cineplastic tragedy that has come out of
his whole nature, a sort of visual symphony as
rich and as complex as the sonorous symphonies
of the great musicians and revealing, by its
precipitation in time, perspectives of infinitude

and of the absolute as exalting by reason of their mystery and more moving because of their reality for the senses, than the symphonies of the greatest of the musicians.

There is the distant future in which I believe, but of which the full realization is beyond my power of imagining. While we await the coming of the cineplast, who is as yet in the shadows of the background, there are today some admirable cinemimics and at least one cinemimic of genius, who are showing us the promise of that collective spectacle which will take the place of the religious dance that is dead, and of the philosophic tragedy that is dead, and of the mystery-play that is dead—indeed of all the great dead things around which the multitude once assembled in order to commune together in the joy that had been brought to birth in the hearts of the people by the mastery over pessimism achieved by the poets and the dancers.

I am not a prophet, I can not tell what will have become in a hundred years of the admirable creations of the imagination of a being, a cinemimic, who, alone among living things, has the privilege of knowing that though his destiny is without hope, he is yet the only being to live and think as if he had the power to take to himself eternity. Yet it seems to me that I already see what the art of that cinemimic may presume to become if, instead of permitting itself to be dragged by theatrical processes through a desolating sentimental fiction, it is able to concentrate itself on plastic processes, around a sensuous and passionate action in which we can all recognize our own personal virtues.

In every land, mankind is attempting to escape from a form of civilization which, through an excess of individualism, has become impulsive and anarchic, and we are seeking to enter a form of plastic civilization that is, undoubtedly, destined to substitute for analytic studies of states and crises of the soul, synthetic poems of masses and great ensembles in action. I imagine that architecture will be the principal expression of this civilization, an architecture whose appearance may be difficult to define—perhaps it will be the industrial construction of our means of travel—ships, trains, automobiles and aeroplanes, for which ports, docks, pontoons, and giant cupolas will be the places of rest and relay.

Cineplastics will doubtless be the spiritual orna-
ment sought for in this period—the play that this
new society will find most useful in developing
in the crowd the sense of confidence, of harmony,
of cohesion.

THE ART OF CHARLIE CHAPLIN

I

WE still speak of giving sight to the blind; but why, if they prefer not to see? For the blind, from generation to generation, are no more desirous of seeing what is before their eyes than those who have sight are weary of seeing. How, then, can we expect the blind to perceive that which has scarcely yet emerged in barest outline and which so few even of those who have eyes to see can understand. For in the cinema we have a new art, the art of movement, an art based on that which is the very principle of everything that exists; an art which is the least conventional of all arts, an immense visual orchestra of which the precursors were the sculptors of the Hindu bas-reliefs and the painters of the drama of lines and of masses in action—Michelangelo, Tintoretto, Rubens, Delacroix; an art which is akin to painting, which moves and renews itself ceaselessly in a visible symphony into which enter the rhythm of the dance and the mysterious changes of a musical poem—enter and sometimes meet and will some day unite. The mechanism of this

art is so directed as to bring before man's eyes
the whole universe of moving form, reconstitut-
ing it for a space in which time precipitates itself,
after man has spiritualized and regulated it in
his heart. It is a new art which has nothing to
do with the theatre. It is a mistake perhaps to
associate it with plastic art. It is still inorganic,
and will not find its true rhythm till society itself
has found its rhythm. How then can we define
it? It is still embryonic. A new art must create
its own organs. All that we can do is to help
to deliver them out of chaos.

So far one man, and only one, has shown that
he entirely understands the new art of the
cinema. Only one man has shown that he knows
how to use this art as if it were a keyboard where
all the elements of sense and feeling that determine the attitude and form of things merge and
convey in one cineographic expression the complex revelation of their inner life and quality.
The master of this new art never speaks, never
writes, never explains. He has no need even to
mask an ephemeral gesture in the conventional
manner of the mimic. In him the human drama
possesses an instrument of expression of which

people hitherto have had no suspicion, an instrument which, in the future, will be the most powerful of all—namely: a screen upon which falls a shaft of light; our eyes look towards it; and behind the eyes, the heart. Nothing more is needed to draw from the heart a wave of new harmonies, a sudden realization of the inevitability of things, and of the everlasting monotonous rhythm of the passions. For there, upon the cinema-screen, are forms that move, faces that reveal, a confused, continuous play of values, lights, and shadows, composing and decomposing unceasingly, uniting the impulses and desires which they express with the feelings and the ideas of the spectator.

Charlie Chaplin is the first man to create a drama that is purely cineplastic, in which the action does not illustrate a sentimental fiction or a moralistic intention but creates a monumental whole; projecting from the inner consciousness a personal vision of the object in a form that is actually visible, in a setting that is actually material and perceptible. There, as it seems to me, we have something very great, an achievement comparable with Titian's concentration of all the sound-elements in time, thus creating from them their very soul and sculpturing it before us. Apparently most people do not perceive this because Chaplin is a clown, and because a poet is, by definition, a solemn person who brings us to knowledge through the door of boredom. Yet to me Chaplin is a poet, even a great poet, a creator of myths, symbols, and ideas, the discoverer of a new and unknown world. I could not even begin to say how much Chaplin has taught me—and always without boring me. Indeed I do not know, for it is too essential to be defined. Every time I see him I have a sense of equilibrium and of certitude which liberates my judgment and sets my ideas swarming. Chaplin reveals to me what is in me, what is truest in me, what is most human. That a man should thus be able to speak to another—is that not strange and unusual?

Somewhere recently I read that Chaplin can not sleep when he is composing one of his dramas, that he is nervous, irritable, distrait or seized with sudden enthusiasm; that it takes him as much as six months to find what it is he wants to do, and then his whole soul strains itself in

the effort of realization. This does not surprise
me. I have read too that Chaplin is thinking
of giving up his work for the cinema; but this
I do not believe. A man who thinks can not, if
he continues to live, give up thinking; and
Chaplin thinks, if I may use such a fearful
adverb, cinematographically; therefore he can
not express his thought except by giving it the
tangible shape of which chance has given him the
symbol. In other words, Chaplin is a
conceptualist. It is his profound sense of reality
which he imposes on all appearances and
movements, upon nature itself, and upon the soul
of men and of objects. He organizes the
universe into a cineplastic poem and flings
forward into the future, in the manner of a god,
this organization which is capable of directing
certain sensibilities and intelligences, and by
means of these, of acting more and more upon
the mind of mankind.

But Chaplin is not merely a cinemime. I am
speaking of the Chaplin of the last two or three
years. Until then he was only a supernumerary
in a sort of circus. The later Chaplin does not
play a part at all. He conceives the universe in

its totality and translates it in terms of the
moving picture. He imagines the drama. He
gives it its laws. He stages it. He plays the
parts of all his associates, as well as his own, and
reunites them all in the final drama after having
explored it and examined it in all its aspects, like
a sculptor shaping and moulding a spherical mass
according to the conception he has formed of it
through his understanding of its projections and
its hollows and the contrasts that result from
them—all the time ceaselessly selecting, com-
bining, and characterizing; or as a musician
controls an orchestra, drawing upon all its tones
and rhythms in order to give infinite variety to
the expression of his grief, joy, surprise or dis-
enchantment.

Chaplin's drama is essentially architectural in
its construction. Each scene is determined by
Chaplin's conception of the whole, just as the
smaller cupolas surround the great central cupola
in the old Byzantine churches, or as music
ordains the song of the spheres and controls the
continuous harmony of their motion. This
architectural quality exists in the brain of
Chaplin and passes with such precision into his

gesture, however extravagant that gesture may seem to be, that it always maintains, as in a rhythmic dance, its equilibrium about the central idea, at once sad and comic, from which it derives its motion.

Chaplin is differentiated from the ordinary comedian—who is but an interpreter of ideas, sentiments, and forms which he has not himself combined—but not from the painter, the architect or the musician, by the camera, the film, and the screen which play the parts of the colors, the brushes, the canvas, the compass, or the instruments of the orchestra. Like a painter, an architect, or a musician, Chaplin enters victoriously into the empire of the poets. See him, the sly elf-like figure dancing out of sight in the shadow of a sordid alley or along the border of a wood—it is Watteau, it is Corot, with the great trees framing the garland of the farandole, the green-blue twilight losing itself under the leaves. See the poor boy as he is carried away in his dream, with his worn-out shoes, his charming, grotesque antics, among the nymphs who dance with him across the sunny meadows. Surrounded by the eternal divinities—the sorceress and the siren,

Hercules and the Minotaur, whom with his little walking-stick and his invincible candor, he drives back into his cave—behold this imp of humanity bringing into association with his humble joy and his absurd suffering, the grand poetic complicity of the winds, the sunshine, the murmuring trees, the reflection of rivers, the plaint of violins.

II

I HAVE said elsewhere that Chaplin makes me think of Shakespeare, and I repeat it, though doubtless many people will regard my insistence with a scornful smile, for this impression forces itself upon me every time I see him. Though he is of less imposing complexity—Chaplin is not yet thirty years old—he has that same bewildering and yet lucid lyricism that Shakespeare had. In the fertility and creativeness of his heart Chaplin has the same limitless fancy which unites in a single gesture an ingenuous delight in the magnificence of life and a smiling, heroic consciousness of its fruitlessness. If Chaplin

leans towards the side of laughter, as Shakespeare does towards the side of lyric ecstasy, it
is, again like Shakespeare, to evade vexatious
reality. Chaplin laughs at himself even while he
suffers, and even while he sings. With unsparing
clarity of vision he watches the freshest effusions
and the most sentimental transports of the heart,
at the moment when they entrust themselves to
the welcoming stars.

Poor Charlot! People love him, and pity him,
and yet he makes them sick with laughter. It is
because he bears within him, like a burden which
he can not lay aside even for an instant—except
when he calls forth from us a joy which helps
him to endure it—the genius that belongs to the
great comic spirits. Like them he has that exquisite imagination which enables him to discover in
every incident and in every act of daily life, a
reason for suffering a little or much, for laughing
at himself a little or much, and for seeing the
vanity that lies beneath the charm and splendor
of appearances. Before Chaplin came we knew
that beneath all drama there is farce, and beneath
all farce there is drama, but what do we not
know now? This man appears, and by his reve-

lation he has taught us to recognize all that we
dimly knew before. His are the simple methods
that belong to greatness: in the midst of danger
an immense distraction seizes him; has he some
great   sorrow?—he   allows   some   grotesque
pleasure to make him forget it; does a lofty
sentiment   fill   his   heart?—man   or   nature
intervenes to make it ridiculous; and if love itself
condemns him to some pathetic gesture he is
overtaken by hiccoughs.

The irony of human passions and of life itself
has so made Chaplin that he sees all things, as
it were, through this irony. Yet the fearful thing
is that he, too, experiences the passions and
desires life. Who can divine his remorse, his
suffering, his exquisite feeling, when, as a poor
man, he silently strips himself for the sake of
one who is poorer than he? Who can realize
his hunger for goodness? He loves, and no one
sees that he loves. He is hungry, and no one
knows that he is hungry. But this does not anger
him; it does not even astonish him; for he sees
himself and can not take himself seriously; and
in order to perceive these contrasts, in revealing
which all his gestures bear the stamp of his comic

power, he has no need to observe the world about
him. These contrasts are within himself; and
his gestures are the discerning expression of the
cruel spectacle which his own thought offers him.

To make these gestures supreme Chaplin has
merely to carry them into the domain of morals
(which determines the progress of his time and
endlessly compares his loftiest illusions with the
sordid reality) and into the infinitely vaster
domain of social and psychological life where
beneath each face, each gesture, each object, the
unseen god watches slyly to plunge a poisoned
dart into the heart of innocence or to humble
it with a smile of triumph, stupidity, or brutality.
. . . Thus, perhaps, Chaplin is fighting; but when
a policeman appears he dances; or while he is
being dragged away by his feet, drunk, he plucks
a flower on the way; or just as he is settling
down to sleep in an open field, he fills up a hole
in a fence in order to stop a draught; or in a
flooded trench, he rolls himself up in his blanket,
yawns, stretches his limbs, and disappears peace-
fully beneath the water; or walking along with
his eyes gazing into the eyes of the beloved, he

falls down a well—but I could go on forever telling these things!

Chaplin's wretchedness—for he is always wretched, this bohemian, this wanderer, this dreamer, this lazy dawdler, so lazy that in order to live he must be ceaselessly imaginative and ingenious, and so simple that in order to realize that a fist is threatening him he must actually feel it on his nose—this wretchedness of his is the canvas on which he paints the golden colors of his wonderful and abounding fancy. We see him carefully deposit his ragged clothes in the great safe of a bank, pull at his imaginary cuffs and regard himself complacently in the non-existent polish of his cracked and broken boots, dust his cane carefully and convey a sense of exquisite elegance by his handling of it, and by his tipping of his shabby old hat down over his eyes. His whole bearing, his manners, bows, and smiles, are those of a complete man of the world, and serve to heighten the contrast with his appearance—shirtless, his rags held together by pins—the amazing silhouette of a tattered dandy. It is a figure which possesses the comic fascination which the Anglo-Saxon genius has revelled in from Shakespeare down to the latest popular clown, as well as a tremendous quality of originality.

What that originality consists of I can not easily say. It is something joyous and yet sombre; a grave imperturbability in the midst of farce; the constant presence, in every gesture, of man's organizing will and the catastrophes of chance. It is the confusion of the visionary before life's drama and his surprise when he is caught up in it, and the pitying return to himself when he finds that he can not escape from it. Chaplin maintains himself on one of the steep summits attained by the genius of man by the unfailing quality of style and distinction which he imprints upon his art. It is an impressive style, which, in the economy of its essentials, is allied with that of the ancient theatre, even while it gives to the personality of the artist a quality of inevitability as irresistible as the march of the days and the seasons, as death and destiny—and yet at the same time it is quite impersonal.

I have spoken of Chaplin's cane and hat, of his boots and his tatters, as unchangeable as the mask and cothurnus of the Greek drama; but what is one to say of his walk, which possesses such a musical rhythm, of his protruding feet, of his leaps of jubilation and lightheartedness, of his despairing staggerings on one heel, of his sudden turns at right angles, of his fantastic steps in moments of danger or when he is fighting, of the silhouette of this droll mechanical clown before which all humanity shakes with laughter?

To sum up, the man who seeks to explain himself to us, does so only when he is telling us of the adventures he has met with in life, and then only if he knows how to relate them—his spiritual adventures, I mean, of course, for only those are of any moment. Chaplin expresses his unfitness for life, which the philosopher knows is every man's unfitness as well; an unfitness for which the artist consoles himself by giving an appearance to his illusions and, with these lost illusions, playing out a heroic farce which he watches as in a mirror. Always beaten, always conquered, Chaplin avenges himself, but always with good temper. He avenges himself by means of jokes or, what is even funnier, by means of blunders which oblige others to bear a part, sometimes the greater part, in his humiliations. When from behind the board-fence he unties the shoe-strings of the policeman who is seeking him, one knows, of course, that he is doing it on purpose, but one is less sure of his intention when he steps on the gouty foot of the man who is persecuting his sweetheart. His innocence and his malice go hand in hand, and by means of his malice he reveals his innocence. When he arrives late at his master's house and submits his poor body to the kick that does not come; when, from his bed, he rattles his wash-basin and drags his shoes about the floor to make his master think that he is getting up, a divine joy fills us, for he is avenging us all, those who have passed and those who are yet to come. Through his resignation and through his vitality he is the conqueror of fate and of despotism. What does death matter, or trouble? He brings laughter through his suffering. The gods flee in all directions.

The gods flee because Chaplin judges impersonally the passion which devastates him; and even if he accepts their domination, he refuses to yield them his respect. Thus he wins the right to judge our passions and to make us face without shame our own infirmity, our own wretchedness and our own despair. He does not laugh at this one or at that one, he laughs at himself and therefore he laughs at us all. A man who can laugh at himself delivers all men from the burden of their vanity, and, as he thus conquers the gods he himself becomes a god to other men. Think of it, Chaplin can make us laugh at hunger itself. His meal at the coffee-stall, his tricks to hide his pilferings and to appear absent-minded and indifferent, even at the moment when his hunger is sharpest, when he is meek and pale with it, and the policeman is approaching; these things draw their comic force from sufferings that seem least suitable for laughter. Why, then, do we laugh, when we ourselves have been hungry, when our children have been hungry? Mainly, I think, especially where the contrast is all the more terrible, because of the victory of the spirit over our own torment. Than this there is nothing which so stamps a man as a man, whether he be a clown or a poet.

This pessimism, constantly conquering itself, makes of this little buffoon a spirit in the great line. The man who never fails to oppose reality

to illusion· and who is willing to play with the
contrast between them is allied, as I have said,
to Shakespeare, and can claim kinship with Montaigne. It is unnecessary to ask whether Chaplin
has read these authors—I have heard that
Chaplin is never without his Shakespeare, but
whether it is true or not he has had no need of
him. For without knowing it one may wear the
features of a most remote ancestor. In any case,
it is the modern spirit, like Shakespeare's, like
Montaigne's, that has guided Chaplin and has
illumined him with the light of dawn: this man,
drunk with intelligence, dancing on the summits
of despair. There is, however, a difference; with
Chaplin the manner of expression is no longer
that of convention; the word is suppressed, and
the written symbol for the word, and even the
sound of it. It is with his feet that he dances,
though they are shod with such incredible wrecks
of leather.

As he hops from one of these feet to the other
—these feet so sad and yet so absurd—he represents the two extremes of the mind; one is named
knowledge and the other desire. Leaping from
one to the other he seeks the centre of gravity

of the soul which he finds only to lose it again immediately. In this search lies the whole of Chaplin's art, as does the art of all great thinkers, of all great artists, and of all those who, without expressing themselves, wish to live deeply and understandingly. If dancing is so close to God, it is, I imagine, because it symbolizes with the most direct gesture and the most invincible instinct, the vertigo of thought which can find its equilibrium only on the hard condition of turning unceasingly about the unstable point which it occupies, of seeking for rest in the drama of movement.

THE TECHNIQUE
OF THE FILM

PUBLICATION No. 1
FILM & SPROCKETS
SOCIETY OF THE CCNY
ART   DEPARTMENT

MARCH 1937

BERNARD GORDON

JULIAN ZIMET

THE TECHNIQUE OF THE FILM

INTRODUCTION 3
DIFFERENTIATING FACTORS 3

PART I— EXPRESSIVE USES OF THE CAMERA

I. CAMERA POSITION 4
    a) For Clarity
    b) Emphasis by Angle
    c) Surprise Effect
II. SIZE DISTORTION 5
    a) Emphasis of a Particular Characteristic
    b) Balance of Power
III. ARRANGEMENT IN PERSPECTIVE 7
IV. DELIMITATION OF THE SCREEN 7
    a) Selection of Detail
    b) Oblique Treatment
V. THE MOVING CAMERA 8
    a) To Center Interest
    b) Subjective Use
VI. THE CREATIVE MANIPULATION OF LIGHT.. 9
    a) Emphasis and Grouping
    b) Plastic Use
    c) To Create Mood
VII. ENLARGING THE FILM VOCABULARY 11

PART II—MONTAGE

DEVELOPMENT 12
I. THE CLOSE-UP FOR EXPOSITION 13
II. FILMIC TIME AND SPACE 14
III. PARALLELISM 14
IV. CONTRAST 15
V. SYMBOLISM 16
VI. RHYTHM 17
VII. ALTERNATIVES TO THE CUT 18
    a) The Fade
    b) The Dissolve
    c) The Wipe

PART III—SOUND

I. THE COMMENTATIVE USE OF SOUND 21
    a) Speech
    b) Natural Sound
    c) Music
II. CONTRASTIVE USE OF SOUND 22
    a) Speech
    b) Natural Sound
    c) Music
III. EVOCATIVE USE OF SOUND 23
    a) Speech
    b) Natural Sound
    c) Music

INTRODUCTION

The attempt to write a concise and simple discussion of the art of the film is inspired by the unfamiliarity with the medium which is apparent even among well educated people. Many who are well acquainted with painting, music and literature are complacently ignorant of the barest fundamentals of cinema construction, although the motion picture affects a large percentage of them even more than the eccepted arts.

On the ground that the film can serve no other function than recording, it has sometimes been denied serious consideration by the academically cultured. The conservatives in the ralm of aesthetics have attributed to the cinema, as sole justification for its existence, an ability to make facsimilies. On that basis, they have condemned it. The purpose of this paper is to establish the contrary premise.

"DIFFERENTIATING FACTORS"

The characteristics of a medium which differentiate it from reality are its fundamental assets. The artist must exploit these "differentiating factors" for expressive ends. One must not regard these factors as hindrances to expression. That would only be the case when the artist was trying to reproduce reality—and then he would not be an artist, but a craftsman. Indeed, the "differentiating factors" are what make an art, if the artist has sufficient control over them to turn them to his own expressive ends.

Let us examine an example of this immediately to make it more clear. Any graphic artist must produce a picture in a chosen space. This flat surface has definite and unchangeable dimensions. Such a condition is obviously different from reality. Human beings have well pivoted eyes and heads which permit them to see a great deal without any conscious delimitation. If the artist's objective were to reproduce reality, this would be a drawback, but since his objective is to represent or interpret reality, we find that the graphic artist takes advantage of this "drawback" and turns it to account. There are three outstanding possibilities for expression which depend upon delimitation of the screen. Thus, the "drawback" of delimitation helps rather than hinders the artist: 1) The edges of the picture permit him to exclude all irrelevant detail; 2) Psychological effects can be created by the reference of horizontal, vertical, and diagonal lines to the borders—restful horizontals, vigorous diagonals, and soaring verticals are used in turn; 3) The screen's frame also opens the possibility of creating meaningful formal compositions through the elements of rhythm, balance, etc.—limitations such as this are invariably associated with successful artistic expression.

A little reflection will yield us several reasons why the screen image is far from a reproduction of reality. It is two dimensional, composed only of reflected light, permanently limited in size and format, observed from a single point of view with distorted perspective, usually in a monochramatic scale, etc. Such limitations are the differentiating factors of the film, i.e., those factors which differentiate the screen image from the world of reality, or nature.

The claim that "the film is a powerful medium, capable of rich and varied expression," must be based on evidence which proves that the filmartist can exploit these factors to mold the material of his environment into a significant form. We shall attempt to prove in this treatise that the film does not reproduce, but represents reality.

Part I—The Expressive Uses of the Camera

I. CAMERA POSITION

As everyone knows, a movie camera is a machine with a single lens, behind which unwinds a roll of film. The image is focussed by the lens on the film strip. When a scene is to be photographed it is up to the director (in this paper we shall continue to use the term "director" in the continental sense, i.e., the person in whose hands are concentrated all the processes of film production, though frequently the duties ascribed to him will actually belong to other film workers such as cameramen, producers, etc.) to choose a position for the camera, i.e., a space relation between the subject and the camera. This relation may be static or dynamic, but in either case there are obviously an infinite number of angles from which to select.

The ubiquitous camera is manifestly not a substitute for the human eye. The individual sees life from a position about five feet above the surface of the earth, occasionally rising above that to look down, rarely dropping below to look up; while the camera, with no apparent exertion of effort, shifts its point of view so that at one moment it looks perpendicularly up from the ground, and at the next, down from the heavens.

If the director aimed only to reproduce reality, he would repudiate this variable camera position and angle. He would restrict himself to those positions which are analogous to one's everyday visual experience. However, desiring to create emotional effects by visual means, he alters his camera position and angle and utilizes change in perspective as an expressive factor.

a) For Clarity

Even the problem of exhibiting an object most clearly is one which involves serious selective processes on the part of the photographer. A simple instance would be the case of photographing a cube. If it were desirable to exhibit the general character of the cube, a position for the camera would be chosen to show three planes. This would indicate, in perspective, that the cube had height, breadth and depth. However, it is equally simple to choose such a relationship between the camera lens and the cube that one face only is visible. Thus the audience cannot determine whether it is viewing a two or three dimensional object. The third dimension, depth, is missing. In this latter instance, the audience cannot appreciate the shape of the solid. If the comparatively simple problem of translating a geometric form into two dimensions makes a demand upon the selective powers of the photographer, it is obvious that the representation of the myriad details of our environment becomes definitely complex.

b) Emphasis By Angle

Just as the director must, on occasion, choose the most characteristic view of a scene, so he must (more often) select a camera position which emphasises a particular quality. Such emphasis serves to clarify meaning and create mood.

Ever since the grapes hung high over the head of the fox, the human race has been afraid that that which is above them will elude their grasp. Unusual significance is invariably attributed to objects which are viewed from below. Thus, in *All Quiet On the Western Front*, when the German lines have been successfully smashed by the French troops, the camera is in one of the shell holes as the great and terrifying figures of the Frenchmen leap over the trenches onto the cringing and defenseless Germans. The psychological effect of this scene is heightened by the upward angle and the proximity of the French soldiers to the camera.

The fact that the audience is forced to see whatever the director wants it to see from whatever point of view he chooses is a 'differentiating factor.' We have seen how the director exploits it.

c) Surprise Effect

In innumerable other instances he constructively employs the differentiating factor of camera position. Sometimes a highly unusual angle is chosen, merely to rivet the audience's attention. Again, a view may be selected to temporarily conceal something which lies behind an obscuring object. This surprise effect is often used for comedy. It is a favorite device of Chaplin's.

In one of his early films there is a scene in which we are introduced to Charlie's parlor. He stands before a picture of his wife, his shoulders heaving convulsively. The camera, behind and below the actor, gives us only enough information to infer that he is sobbing for his run-away spouse. A sudden shift of the camera reveals the cause of his contortions, a cocktail-shaker held firmly in his hands. The effect is irresistibly hilarious. The most comprehensive point of view was rejected in this instance because of the expressive possibilities of the unusual camera position.

II. SIZE DISTORTION

There is a universal law of optics to the effect that the size of an object varies inversely with the square of the distance. This is true for all optical mechanisms including the human eye. Therefore, when an individual is watching two men five and ten feet away respectively, the figure of the latter makes an image on the retina which is one fourth the size of the image of the former. The individual is never tempted to believe that the nearer man is four times larger than the farther one. His brain cooperates with his eye to arrive at the understanding that both men are approximately of the same size. Similarly, when objects at different distances from the camera are in juxtaposition on the screen, the size relationship is distorted. It is true that the spectator reinterprets this relationship, just as he does in life, but a great degree of emphasis still remains.

Such photographic distortion is best exemplified by a favorite trick of the amateur photographer. We have all seen snapshots in which the subject's legs were extended directly towards the camera. The resulting photograph is one in which the feet are enormously enlarged in relation to the rest of the body. Under natural circumstances, we frequently encounter just such a condition (an individual's feet extended towards us) but we never notice the relative magnification of the feet. This is due, as we have mentioned, to the interpretive action of the brain. The fact that the camera lens does not interpret, explains the distortion in the snapshot, and is one of the differentiating factors of photography. The size relationships of objects in three dimensional space are distorted by the photographic lens.

a) Emphasis of a Particular Characteristic

Whereas the above example is so crude and obvious as to lack any artistic significance, it does point the way along which genuine expressive efforts may be directed. In the film, *Frankenstein,* during a murder, a somewhat

—5

routine exercise for the inhuman monster of the film, a tremendously vivid impression was conveyed by a slight distortion of the hands of the murderer. The camera was placed before and below him, so that when he extended his claw-like hands to strangle his victim, the enlarged tentacles seemed to hover over the audience. Strong men closed their eyes and women fainted. What would have been merely another insipid execution (if the action had been photographed without this distortion) was transformed into a gruesome spectacle by the judicious utilization of the differentiating factor of size distortion.

b) Balance of Power

In the above example we observed how this type of distortion was used to emphasize a specific part of a single object (the hand of the monster). Even more frequently, such distortion is employed to distinguish among several objects, emphasizing some over others. The axiom is "Importance varies directly with size."

Consider the problem before the film artist in this case. The action to be photographed is the shelling of a coastal city by ships off-shore. Of all the possible points of view, the most obvious one is the 'profile.' The profile image projected would reveal the ships at the extreme left of the screen and the city at the extreme right. In order to photograph both at once, it would be necessary to remove the camera so far from the material that the resultant discrepancy in size between city and ships would misplace emphasis. The diminutive fleet would be negligible in comparison with the large areas occupied by the city, and the importance of the batteries would be underestimated. The technical limitations of the film would, in such a case, have overwhelmed the film-artist.

However, a competent film-worker who appreciated the expressive possibilities of this particular factor of his medium, would have proceeded differently. One method is this. The camera is so placed that the city, the cannon and the lens form a straight line in that order. The camera is aboard ship, directly behind the guns. Since the cannon are very much closer to the camera than is the city in question, the former will occupy the major portion of the screen and will loom there menacingly. The increase in the significance of the guns (through increase of relative size) affects the interpretation of the scene. The new and increased effect of the shot* owes its power to the factor of size distortion of the photographic lens. Precisely this procedure was employed by Eisenstein in the epoch-making *Potemkin* during the shelling of Odessa.

The limiting case of such distortion is that in which the nearest object completely fills the screen. The obliteration of subject matter by interposing an object between it and the lens offers striking symbolical possibilities. Matter swallowing up matter suggests the concept of destruction. In the film *The General Died At Dawn* (Lewis Milestone), this effect was achieved. We see a rolling countryside which war tanks and artillery are traversing. Suddenly, a tank cuts across the field of vision and obscures the view as it proceeds across the screen. The forces of war are simply and effectively symbolized as destroying the country-side.

---

* A "shot" is the action portrayed on a strip of film which has passed through the camera without interruption, e.g., let us say that we take a "shot" of a character who is six feet from the camera. If it is then desirable to change the material on the screen to say a "close-up" shot of his feet, the camera is stopped and the scene

III. ARRANGEMENT IN PERSPECTIVE

The factor of camera position is often employed by the director to create relationships between objects included within the shot.

In the Russian film, *The Ghost that Never Returns*, by Alexander Room, the director was faced with the problem of representing the release of a convict. He selected an interesting relationship between the camera, the man and the prison gate. The camera remained behind the bars of the gate as the man walked down a long alley on the outside. The network of bars extended across the screen as the man walked away. This relationship emphasized the permanency of the institution. The director might have used a number of alternate camera positions. A bird's-eye-view would have included all the necessary material, but the presentation would have been less effective. If the camera had been facing the prison with the convict in the foreground, the importance of the man would have been emphasized. Again, he might have shot the scene so that only the prisoner and the open countryside were visible, with the prison behind the camera. This last would have completely minimized the importance of the institution.

In the shot taken through the gate, the connection between the prison and the individual was made apparent. The network of bars across the screen remained as a permanent barrier between the convict and the spectator. The relationship between the bars and the man was such as to emphasize the lasting effect of the institution upon the convict.

IV. DELIMITATION OF THE SCREEN

In the preceding sections we considered the differentiating factors of camera position and size distortion of the photographic lens. Examples were given to illustrate the creative exploitation of these differentiating factors. We shall now turn our attention to another factor, the "delimitation of the screen," i.e., the simple fact that the screen has a definite and unchangable size and shape. (*See Page* 3)

a) Selection of Detail

One of the most widely used methods of art is the selection of significant detail. In the film, the fact that the borders of the screen may be used to exclude irrelevant matter, permits the film artist to concentrate the attention of the audience on any detail, though it be but the size of a pin. The director can shift the camera from one object to another with perfect ease, and in this manner can force upon the attention of the audience whatever he considers necessary for the proper development of the film, and can exclude all that he considers superfluous. Here is a power of selection which among all the arts, is available only to the literary artist and the film director.

In the *Love of Jeanne Ney*, by Pabst, this use of the close-up is admirably demonstrated. The following is a conspicuous example. A fat, baldheaded miser is seated at a table going through the motions of counting an enormous sum of money. As a matter of fact, his hands are empty, but he imagines that he is counting a pile of bank-notes. Through autosuggestion, he works himself into a frenzy of satiated avarice. In rapid succession, close-

---

rearranged for the second "shot." When several such "shots" are combined (the number is arbitrary) to form a dramatic unit, they are referred to as a "sequence", a term approximating "scene" in the theatre.

up shots of his popping eyes, slobbering lips and convulsively agitated fingers are projected on the screen. Thus, a complex emotional situation is clearly delineated by a choice of salient detail.

b) Oblique Treatment

The value of an oblique or suggestive treatment is universally recognized, and the graphic differentiating factor of the film which we are now considering permits something of this nature. Sometimes in pursuance of this obliquity, in order to heighten the suggestive power of a scene, it is desirable to show the effect of an object rather than the object itself. The cause, out of sight, is emphasized by showing only its effect within the margins of the screen.

Every time we see an individual on the screen who is reacting to some unseen stimulus, we are witnessing an application of delimitation. In almost any mystery thriller, a scene similar to the following occurs: On the screen, only the gentle heroine is visible. We see her start suddenly at something beyond the borders of the screen. As her terror grows, we realize that whatever is frightening her is coming closer. A strong feeling of suspense is gradually created, and when the murderer finally appears upon the screen, his entrance is heightened in its dramatic effect. This climax, created by the concealment of the murderer until the crucial moment, is an oblique treatment which depends upon the differentiating factor of screen delimitation.

V. THE MOVING CAMERA

In introducing the subject of CAMERA POSITION, we mentioned that the relation between the camera and the subject might be either static or dynamic. So far, we have dealt exclusively with considerations of the static position of the camera. The dynamic, or moving camera, is another of the differentiating factors of the film.

a) To Center Interest

Frequently, in a given sequence, the center of interest is an object in motion—a moving automobile, a running child, etc. If it is desirable to keep this moving object on the screen for any appreciable length of time, it is apparent that the camera will have to move along with it. The most obvious use of the moving camera is to keep up with a moving object in order to prevent it from shifting off the screen. *Potemkin* provides an excellent example of how this technique can be utilized dramatically. In the scene of the massacre on the Odessa steps, a mother, wheeling a perambulator, is shot dead. The carriage teeters on the edge of the steps and slowly, with horrible indecision, begins to career down the stone stairs. It moves jerkily, convulsively, and with gathering momentum. The defenseless infant in its carriage, traveling in a broken rhythm toward certain death, symbolizes the inhumanity of the slaughter. This "truck" (any bodily movement of the camera) was made because the carriage was properly the center of interest throughout the duration of its movement. If attention was merely to be attracted to a carriage rolling down the steps, it would have been sufficient for us to see a shot of the carriage starting down and a second shot as it stopped. But since the very manner in which the carriage moved was dramatic, it was necessary and proper for the camera to accompany it.

When the sole purpose of a "truck" is to indicate that an object is moving from one point to another, the device is misapplied because no expressive end is served. It is simpler merely to indicate in one shot that the mobile object is leaving and in the next shot to show its arrival at the destination. In this way the time consumed in accompanying it is saved and an irrelevancy eliminated. Economy is always desirable. The moving camera must have definite expressive ends, otherwise its motion is a meaningless device and the audience finds itself forced to religiously trail such undramatic objects as automobiles, pedestrians and elevators.

b) Subjective Use

Thus far, the camera has represented the impersonal and all-seeing eye. It has played the role of the author of a book written in the third person. This is the "objective" use of the camera. It is equally simple to make the lens represent the eye of an actor and thus become an instrument for a first person description. Then the camera is used "subjectively."

An interesting, though extreme example of this technique comes from *The Last Laugh,* by F. W. Murnau. The protagonist, Emil Jannings, has been to a wedding feast where he has imbibed too freely. The director wished to portray the effects on the old man. In order to do this, the photographer strapped the camera to his chest and staggered about the room. The drunkeness of the old man was vividly portrayed as we viewed, through his befuddled senses, the shocking behavior of the properties on the set.

Another example of the creative use of camera movement, one employing the "tilt" rather than the "track," comes from the vigorous British school of documentary film workers. Stuart Legg, in producing *Telephone Workers* wished to create the impression of the rapid growth of modern towns which necessitated the extension of telephone communications. He brilliantly conceived the idea of pointing the camera to the sky over a typical town and slowly tilting the camera downwards. This process was repeated several times from different locations. First appeared the sky; then one or two buildings, pushing their way through the bottom and working up into the center of the screen in a manner strongly suggestive of spontaneous biologic growth. The sum total effect of the shots was that of a rapid "mushroom" growth, which was exactly the director's intention. In this instance, the film artist succeeded in presenting one of those generalizations which are ordinarily so difficult to express in the film.

This ingenious device is an example of an expressive use of the moving camera which does not fit into either of the above categories. Directors, in solving the problems that arise during production, frequently invent such expressive techniques, which, in the aggregate, result in the growth of the power of the medium.

VI. THE CREATIVE MANIPULATION OF LIGHT

We all know that film images are composed of light which is reflected from the screen. In most present day films, we deal with white light and a scale of grays which shade off to black. This reduction of the artist's multicolored material to a monochromatic scale is an unnatural condition which is but one more of the differentiating factors with which we deal. As all the others have been profitably exploited, so has this. Light and shade are to the photographer, in a sense, what color is to the painter.

a) Emphasis and Grouping

The camera transforms all the colors of the natural world into a scale of grays in a manner which is subject to exact physical laws with which the director must be well acquainted. He knows in advance that the reds, greens, blues, etc., of the set are to be transposed into various shades of gray, and he can make use of this knowledge to determine the light distribution which will finally appear on the screen (the chiaroscuro). This control over the disposition of light and shade permits the film artist to emphasize, minimize, group and separate objects. If an object contrasts with the rest of the shot by virtue of a striking difference in light value, it will obviously be emphasized, e.g., something dark in a light setting or vice versa. Illumination from the side will cast shadows between masses and will serve to separate them. The elimination of such shadows by a flat front lighting will bring the components into a closer relationship.

b) Plastic Use

There is a related but somewhat different plastic function of lighting which the director must employ. This is that the photographer can change the shape of his subject by the proper regulation of light values. Every individual who has had his photograph taken has remarked on the fact that he appears more handsome or less ugly in one picture than in another. The features have not changed in the interval between photographs, but the lighting conditions have. The photographer can mold the face by placing lights in various positions. Thus, a strong illumination from the side makes a long, melancholy looking countenance appear shorter, rounder and more jovial; a light placed directly above the head tends to have the contrary effect.

It is common knowledge that movie stars seldom look the same on the screen as they do in life. Most readers of "fan" magazines are aware, too, that many of the stars insist on having one special cameraman work on their films. The reason for this is that the artificial studio lighting is controlled so as to achieve the most flattering effect, and once a cameraman has learned the technique of complimenting a star's appearance, she (or he) is often unwilling to risk a picture with a strange cameraman who may not be so successful in the subtle art of flattery—with Klieg lights.

There is a superb example of the creative use of this technique in that touching French film La Maternelle. We have been introduced to a pitiful little fellow who is revoltingly ugly, apparently as a result of malnutrition. In the course of the film, we have come to understand him as a waif who has suffered all the evil influences of the Paris gutter. He responds to the loving influence of his teacher and becomes an amenable child. He dies, and his mother, in speaking of it at the day school where the young teacher works, conjures up an image of the child. Here, the director permits us to look for a moment at the child through loving eyes, and by a miraculous transformation of lighting, we see the touching portrait of an almost beautiful child. This instance is one of exceptional excellence, but it is a commonplace to see characters change from haggard and drawn creatures to fresh ones, etc.

c) To Create Mood

Color is known to have a direct influence upon mood. This is due to the psychological associations between color and emotion. Red and yellow are warm, vibrant colors. Blue is cool and restful, etc. There are fairly obvious explanations for this which need not concern us. Let it suffice that we recognize the empiric fact that we make such distinctions in the emotional interpretation of color. Our reaction to light and shade is analagous to our response to color stimuli. Light and dark have always symbolized joy and gloom. This reaction has roots which are irrevocably entwined in the human make-up.

Because the film artist has control over the variety of contrast and the intensity of light in any shot, he has a hand on the well-springs of our emotions. This power is universally recognized and audiences are quick to discern and appreciate its application. A simple example of this is the use of the "high key" shot. "High key" is used to describe a shot in which the scale of values is from medium gray to white. There are no dark grays, blacks, or strong contrasts in the picture. These shots with their subtle gradations and almost imperceptible nuances of light are employed for scenes of fragile beauty; in Hollywood, children playing, or virgins praying.

"Low key" shots are even more frequently employed. In low key work, the shades run from medium gray to black, without any highlights. The effect of such shots is naturally the opposite of the effects achieved in high key work. Instead of "fragile beauty," we feel gloom, impending sorrow, dangerous brooding, etc. Whole pictures are sometimes pitched in low key. These are the "screen tragedies." An example which effectively demonstrates this technique is *The Informer,* which owed much of its effects to photographic lighting.

VII. ENLARGING THE FILM VOCABULARY

The film is rigidly limited in its ability to express general concepts. Consider the difficulty, or rather, the impossibility of expressing in terms of filmic images, the following stanza of poetry:

> *It breaks his heart that kings must murder still,*
> *That all his hours of travail here for men*
> *Seem yet in vain, and who will bring white peace*
> *That he may sleep upon his hill again?*
> ABRAHAM LINCOLN WALKS AT MIDNIGHT
> —Vachel Lindsay

For words such as: hour, here, seem, yet, in vain, and, who, his, thus, etc., etc., which are indispensable to the writer, there are no visual counterparts. Such words are necessary to any generalized expression. Without them, abstractions are impossible. If, in writing, we were to limit ourselves to picture words, that is, nouns and verbs which conjure up only simple visual images, we would begin to have difficulty with simple narration, not to mention exposition. Primitive language was mainly nominal. The aggregate efforts of many human generations striving for expression brought adjectives, adverbs and abstract verbs into the language. One of the most important functions of the film worker is that of discovering new devices which will add to the maturity and sophistication of the language of the film. Concrete images must be made the vehicles for abstractions and generalized descriptions. The camera sees only concrete physical objects and so must depend on their arrangement for expressing abstract and subtle ideas. Most of the examples described in these pages deal with the successful filmic representation of such abstract concepts.

—11

Part II—Montage

DEVELOPMENT

Until now we have been trying to acquaint the reader with the film director's problems in producing single shots. We will now turn our inquiry to the methods used to integrate shots into a sequence.

In the earliest beginnings of film making, the "continuous" method of shooting was employed. At that time it was necessary to prepare and rehearse the entire action so that when the camera was placed in position and the film started, the shooting continued until the episode was completed. This technique is exemplified in the earliest Edison films. In these, we see action recorded exactly as it occurred. Each film was a complete, continuous whole, similar to a skit on the stage. Because there were no breaks in the continuity, the scope of the film was restricted to those subjects which could be photographed in one place and in a few minutes.

To overcome this difficulty, the early film workers devised the process of splicing. Thus a film of any length could be shot by splicing the separate rolls of film end to end.

Which lets the cat out of the bag. That wonderful mysterious cliche, "montage." is scratching at the door. Splicing was the forerunner of "montage." There is nothing abstruse about the process itself, though its use determines the nature of filmic expression. The word "montage" is French, and literally means "assemblage—putting together," coming from the verb "monter," which means "to assemble." The single physical fact about the process of montage is that strips of film of varying length are pasted end to end (spliced) so that the result is a length of film which is a composite of any number of individual strips or shots.

Once the obstacle of time limitation had been overcome, the early film workers looked about for more adequate story material, and found it in the drama.

The drama offered them ready-made scenarios (scripts) which they proceeded to photograph with little or no alteration.

There was no difficulty in shooting individual scenes (or episodes). This process was merely an amplification of the old "one incident" nickelodeon. The camera was set up at the scene of action and ground away until the actors completed the scene. However, in the modern drama, the interval between scenes is employed to represent a lapse of time and a change in locale. Thus, the film workers who were attempting to reproduce a drama had no difficulty so long as they were shooting individual scenes, but they faced a new problem when they came to the curtain intermissions.

This gap between scenes was bridged with titles.

As the public became acclimated to the new, freer film, the demand for titles to explain such simple shifts in time and space decreased. For example, on the morning of a marriage, a shot in the bride's home could be followed immediately by a scene in the groom's home without any intervening titles. It became possible to continue scene upon scene without interruption.

Once it became possible to juxtapose scenes, it was but a step to the complete unrestricted discontinuity of the modern film. We can now select details *within* the scene and present them to the audience in any desired succession.

Let us examine a rough scenario of a simple sequence. What occurs is that a man walks around the corner of a house, stops in front of it and calls someone in a second storey window. A woman looks out and a conversation ensues. We see a man round the opposite corner of the house. When he sees what is occurring, he slinks back, picks up a rock and hurls it at the first man . . . This is not a scenario, but a bare narration of what occurs. In shooting such a sequence, the director could conceivably decide to take the whole arena of action and merely grind away while the events were being enacted, in a theatrical manner. This is rarely, if ever, done. Instead we may get:

1. A long shot of the house.
2. A medium shot of the first man who is coming around the left corner of the house.
3. A close-up of his face.
4. A medium shot as he cranes his neck to call up to the window.
5. A tilting shot up the wall of the house stopping at the desired window.
6. Shot inside house: woman as she approaches window.
7. Outside shot: woman as she looks down from window.
8. A long shot as No. 1 showing the man and woman in relation to each other. We first notice the figure of the second man at right corner of house.
9. A medium shot of second man as he slinks back.
10. Big close-up of his face as it is contorted with rage.
11. Big close-up of his hand as he grasps a rock on the ground.
12. Big close-up of first man's head as it turns upon noticing second man, etc., etc.

The remarkable thing about this scenario, the thing that strikes us immediately when comparing it with early action melodramas, is this: The camera is no longer reproducing objects as they move before it. Life has been injected into the camera. It has become the eye of an observer taking active part in the action—an observer who moves about viewing the actions from behind, from above, from below—an observer upon whose brain is flashed the important details as they become significant—who sees first a man walking, and then concentrates upon his peculiar facial expression. An observer who sees a man look up, and who then turns to follow his gaze. One who sees the man call up to the window, then dashes upstairs in a thousandth part of a second to see the woman go to answer. A great difference between the old, static, continuous method and this. It is immediately clear that the technique adopted is greatly superior to the old continuous method. The scenario outlined above demonstrates a technique for the selection and emphasis of detail, which, for practical purposes of exposition, is unique.

I. THE CLOSE-UP FOR EXPOSITION

This technique depends mainly upon the close-up, the function of which is to direct the attention of the spectator to that detail which is, at the moment, significant. The succession of close-ups, such as the man's hate contorted face, followed by the shot of his hand grasping a stone, demonstrates the ability of the film, through this discontinuous method, to select and emphasize. While these shots are on the screen, all the rest of the action, (the man and woman talking, etc.) is withdrawn from the spectator's attention. The selection of details, the man's face and the hand on the stone, create vividly and succinctly the impression of the man's emotional state and his objective reaction.

II. FILMIC TIME AND SPACE

In distorting "real" time and space, the director creates a new "filmic time and space." The completed motion picture is a cosmos in itself, wherein all the ordinary laws of dimensions are flagrantly disregarded. For example, when it is necessary to show that an individual is crossing the street, the movie director can take one shot as he leaves the curb, followed immediately by a second as the actor enters a house on the other side of the street. A few undramatic seconds have been eliminated. In this particular instance, there is a concentration of natural time. It is equally simple to distort nature in the opposite manner, i.e., to expand time. It is possible for the director to grasp a single significant moment and maintain it until its full dramatic value has been exploited. This is done by representing, in consecutive shots, actions that occur simultaneously. For example: A bandit draws a revolver and threatens a group of people. The scenario is: 1) A long shot of the man drawing his pistol; 2) A long shot of the group of victims; 3, 4, 5, 6) A series of consecutive close-ups showing the parallel expressions on the faces of each of the members of the group. The representation on the screen would take about ten seconds, whereas, in reality, the action would be over in two seconds. The normal progression of time and action has been arrested to show all the important simultaneously occurring events.

On the stage, it is no more possible to expand the moment than to eliminate the irrelevant action of the actor crossing the street. This demonstrates the difference between stage and screen representation of time and space. Within the confines of any one scene, it is impossible for the dramatist to be discontinuous, whereas the film artist can entirely remold or recreate temporal and spatial dimensions.

III. PARALLELISM

So far, we have considered the use of montage to show details within a single scene (the hold up). Montage is also featured in the selection and juxtaposition of details from disconnected scenes. This was touched upon before during the discussion of discontinuity, and the example of the alternate shots of bride and groom was given. A further development of this technique resulted in the editing of entire sequences in such a manner. In Griffith's *Intolerance*, the fundamental discontinuity of the film was thus employed to present three parallelly developing themes.

An innocent man, unjustly condemned to die, is in the prison deathhouse awaiting execution. Many miles away, an automobile bearing evidence to free him is racing to catch an express train on which the Governor is travelling. The shots on the screen are alternately of the preparations for the execution, the speeding car, and the express train. As the time for the execution draws near, the camera cuts rapidly back and forth among the three developing threads of action. This technique creates a state of great tension, which, by the time that the spectacular rescue is accomplished, has developed ino a very dramatic climax. This is another example of heightened expression which depends upon the differentiating factor of film discontinuity.

There are some difficulties attendant upon this process which shoud be glanced at in passing. In order that the relation between the shots be comprehensible, there is usually a link of form or content. This link may be a central theme which continues throughout the series of shots. For example, if a film were to begin with consecutive shots of a train, an automobile, a ship and an aeroplane, a unity would exist. The central idea of transportation is clear, and each of the shots is accepted as contributing towards that concept. If instead, the audience were to be greeted with a heterogeneous assortment of shots, e.g., a mountain, a hand and a shoe, the resulting confusion would be obviously due to the lack of a binding theme. Ordinarily, the flow of the story is sufficient to explain such cross-cutting as that employed by Griffith in the reprieve sequence. However, it frequently occurs that the intellectual relationship between shots is obscure.

Suppose that a war film were to begin in the trenches at the front and then cut to the distant home of a soldier. If the shot of the battlefield were to be immediately followed by a shot of the apartment, without any previous introduction or explanation, some confusion would undoubtedly be created. In order to clarify the relationship between the soldier and his home, and to smooth the abrupt spatial transfer, the director employs the device of parallel forms. Thus the first shot would be one in which the helmet of the soldier plays a prominent and shiny part. The next shot will disclose the kitchen of the home, in which a pot, hanging on the wall, occupies the same position on the screen as the helmet did before. The similarity of the two objects serves to associate the diverse shots and permits the audience to transfer its attention from the war torn front to the distant homes without much difficulty. Such purely structural similarity, either in the composition or in the shape of a detail, eases the transition.

The application of montage to select and emphasize details from disconnected scenes, as well as from within individual scenes, has widened considerably the scope of the film. Its essential discontinuity permits and encourages the development of plot by the counterpoint of independent themes.

IV. CONTRAST

Contrast is an important element in all artistic expression. It is one of the devices with which the artist heightens impressions. Each medium has its characteristic methods. In the drama, emphasis may be achieved by two actors in contrasting emotional states. Thus, to emphasize the agitation of Hamlet at the appearance of his father's ghost, the Spirit is usually calm and deliberate in voice and gesture. Similarly, other arts use contrasting colors, words, sounds, lines, etc., for emphasis and distinction.

The film, too, employs kindred devices within the shot. However, it is another distinctive type of contrast which depends upon montage. This is the contrast of juxtaposed images. What could be more effective than to have violently opposed images flashed in instantaneous succession on the screen?

An obvious application of this exists in the emphasis of form through contrast. A graceful dancer becomes yet more graceful when preceded by awkwardness personified. The dimensions of "fat" and "skinny" (Laurel and Hardy) are emphasized by their contrast.

More significant is the contrast of the ideological and emotional content of successive shots. In the labor-produced documentary film *Millions of Us*, the entire theme is built around the contrast of the want and plenty which exist side by side. An unemployed man who has assuaged his hunger with sleep, dreams of luscious fruits, succulent steaks, mountains of bread . . . Shots of starving, ill-clad people are interlaced with shots of the ruthless destruction of consumer goods. The film thus becomes a medium for the

—15

succinct and powerful exposition of ideas.

Emotional contrast can be achieved by the juxtaposition of shots which inspire different moods. Gloomy, low-key shots may be placed before light, airy ones in order to evoke an appropriate response. This evocative technique is employed in *Maid of Salem*, which uses numerous contrasts of high and low-key shots. A good example from this picture is the instance when the women have been listening to the tall tales of a Negro slave. Suddenly, the stern puritanical "elder" appears. He breaks up the group of "evil" gossipers. The women are driven through the bright outdoor sunlight into the sudden gloom of the Puritan home. The abrupt contrast of dark against light causes the audience to respond instantly to the depression which seized the brow-beaten women.

There is a further development of filmic contrast which is strikingly effective because of the introduction of a refinement. Instead of merely presenting two conflicting abstractions (want vs. plenty, hunger and food), the director chooses objects which represent the abstractions, but which, in addition, resemble each other in form. A shot of hands raking in winnings on a gaming table may be followed by a shot of a different pair of hands picking scraps of food from a garbage can. The fact that the abstractions (of poverty and affluence) are form-linked, brings to mind more sharply the involved differences.

Such contrast of ideas, emotions and forms used to heighten the expressive qualities of the medium, is only possible because of the absence of the space-time continuum. This differentiating factor accounts for an expressive technique which is peculiarly appropriate to the film medium.

V. SYMBOLISM

Charley Chaplin's *Modern Times* opens with a shot of flocks of sheep closely packed, pushing, crowding, senselessly impelled onward. The next shot is of a similar "flock" of modern men and women closely packed . . . "senselessly impelled onward." This type of montage, in which there is a comparison (created by juxtaposition) between something in the context of the film and an ideal symbol (the sheep) which is outside the context of the film, is exactly analogous to the simile construction of the writer. This device adds the word "like" to the vocabulary of the film.

Another closely related use of symbolism, we may term the "metaphor." In this construction, the director remains within the context of the film. He uses as symbols, material which normally occurs in the environment of the scene. For instance, if he wishes to poetically portray a love affair, the "simile" method would be to film the lovers in a living room, and then cut in shots of amorous birds, streams running to meet the sea, bees extracting nectar from flowers, etc. There is a distinct danger, though, that such interpolation will be confusing. An alternate method, which at once avoids this confusion and achieves greater subtlety, would be to have the two lovers walking in the woods and fields. The camera can turn up to the boughs of trees to see the birds; it can turn aside to watch the junction of two brooks; it can, finally, avert its gaze from the lovers to watch the bee and the pollen laden flower.

The simile and the metaphor, then, have been added to the list of expressive devices of the film. It is by such a process of innovation and discovery, by the invention of competent film workers, that a medium as young as this grows rich and expressive.

VI. RHYTHM

One of the most interesting and, certainly, important developments of montage is "rhythm." Webster defines rhythm as "movement marked by regular recurrence." In what sense can the film create such rhythm? To what "movement" do we refer when discussing "rhythmical montage"?

It will be recalled that the fundamental unit of film construction is the shot. Each shot is a brick which is used in the construction of a complete edifice, the film. These shots vary in length and content. Each one, therefore, has a definite "weight" in relation to the others. It is roughly analagous to the syllable in poetry. Movement is created by the succession of shots (there may be over two thousand shots in a picture). These vary in length from a fraction of a foot to any number of feet, and by the proper arrangement of short and long shots the director may create slow, fast, rising, or falling tempos. A series of short shots creates rapid movement; long ones, slow movement. This type of filmic "movement" strongly influences the mood of the spectator.

Rapid movement always evokes excitement. Slow movement tends to create a state of relaxation. Therefore, when there is flashed in rapid succession a series of short staccato shots, the audience reacts excitedly. Conversely, a series of long shots (slow filmic movement), will create a quiet mood. In addition to these "absolutes" of fast and slow movement, there is the important concept of acceleration and deceleration. Filmic acceleration means that the shots grow progressively shorter so that the movement is speeded up. This creates a growing state of tension. Deceleration, a lengthening of the successive shots, results in a gradual relaxation from strain.

An excellent example of rapid cutting to create rising emotion is seen in the finale of *Janosik*. The protagonist, a Slovak Robin Hood, has been condemned to death by hanging from the ribs on a hook. He is performing a danse-macabre on the gallows as a final gesture of defiance. An already tense sequence is made almost unbearable by a rising tempo. At first, slowly, we see different shots of the dancing figure, the hook, the judges who have just sentenced him, the group of musicians who are playing his favorite folk song, the crowd of spectators who wait . . . The shots grow shorter. We are whirled past dancing feet, sweating faces, judges, hook, instruments, spectators—around again—still faster, until finally, he throws himself upon the hook. The cut is made before he is actually impaled. The next shot is a long serene one of feathery clouds racing across the sky, with a suggestion of Janosik's beloved mountains in the foreground. This last shot, in such contrast to the agitated tempo of the preceding ones, permits the spectator to regain his composure and to realize that Janosik's death has not been a tragedy, but rather, the ultimate sublimation of a glorious career.

Raymond Spottiswoode offers an interesting explanation of the audience reaction caused by the Janosik sequence. When a new shot is flashed on the screen, it has a definite intellectual and formal content that must be absorbed by the audience, i.e., each shot represents an idea (or a step in the development of an idea), and in addition has a graphic composition which the spectator explores. Therefore, when a new shot is first projected, the audience becomes more attentive. Its receptivity is increased, and with it, all sense rections. As soon as the spectators have absorbed the main substance of the shot, they lapse into their customary lethargy. If the shot is held too long, they become actively bored and impatiently await the next. We have never heard of a shot being shouted off the screen, but we have, on occasion, wished to do just that, because it was held on the screen beyond the point when it was of any significance or interest. A shot with complicated forms, motions and ideas, in order to be comprehensible, must be held longer than one with a single simple subject.

If the sequence of shots, then, is one with a gradually rising tempo, as the shots grow shorter, the audience has less and less opportunity to relax between shots. Caught each time at a higher point of attention, the audience's sense reactions are raised to the desired pitch. Conversely, when the shots are being lengthened (diminuendo), the spectator is permitted to gradually relax. More time is allowed him to examine each consecutive shot. Each one finds him at a "lower" point, until finally he is completely relaxed and can watch the progress of the film composedly. Long shots, then, tend to evoke moods which are appropriate to quiet inactive scenes, while short ones are properly employed for animated movement and action.

We see that with this technique of "rhythmical montage" the director has control of an important expressive device. Once again, the characteristic discontinuity of the film has accounted for a significant creative agency of the medium.

If the reader will glance again at the dictionary definition of rhythm, he will observe that the element of movement must be modified by "periodicity, regular recurrence"; in other words, the organization of a pattern. This is an expressive factor to be found in all dynamic arts. Thus, in poetry, different types of feet, and their variations, are employed to express mood. The filmic possibilities of this method are still largely theoretical.

From a simple physical process, originally employed to increase the length of motion pictures, we have seen develop an impressive array of expressive devices. The technique of selection and emphasis, which is peculiar to the film, ultimately depends upon splicing. Parallelism, the contrapuntal development of themes, also owes its existence to the discontinuity of the medium. So, too, with contrast, symbolism, and filmic rhythm—all derive from the method of joining shots, of counterpoising them, and of weaving them into patterns.

The differentiating factor of discontinuity, the factor which makes of the film something so different from reality, the factor which the direcor exploits to create a new "filmic time and space," is responsible for the expressive technique which distinguishes the medium.

VII. ALTERNATIVES TO THE CUT

We have thus far assumed that the reader has a general understanding of the term "cut." This was, for purposes of exposition, a convenient assumption. A "cut" is a theoretical concept, just as is a mathematical line, or point, or the "edge" which separates two areas. A "cut" has no more existence than these mathematical symbols; it is but the term used to denote the transition from one shot to the next. For practical purposes, there is no real dimension to the interval between shots. One shot follows another in uninterrupted progression. This quality of free cinematic "motion," the unrestricted juxtaposition of shots, we have indicated to be the foundation of film construction. Because it maintains and emphasizes this discontinuity, the cut is the proper, and, necessarily, the primary method of transition between shots.

a) The Fade

There are, however, some alternatives to the cut which are occasionally useful. The "fade-out" and "fade-in" are used to separate sequences. The terms "fade-out" and "fade-in" are self-descriptive. In this device, the screen image which concludes the sequence grows dark to indicate the termination of the sequence. The next shot starts with the screen almost completely dark (as it was left by the "fade-out" shot) and "fades-in" by means of an increasing luminosity, until it has built up its full light intensity.

The "fade" creates the feeling that the successive shots are spatially, temporally and ideologically remote, and, as such, is similar to the curtain drop of the theatre. Although the "fade" was the only device used to express discontinuity in the early film, it is seldom used in the modern film except for the initial "fade-in" and "final fade-out."

b) The Dissolve

The "dissolve," "lap-dissolve," or "mix,' is a device which derives from the fade. However, before the first shot has "faded out", the second shot "fades in." It starts to appear as soon as the first shot begins to "fade." Halfway through the dissolve there are two equally bright superimposed images. The first shot "fades out" completely just as the second assumes full intensity.

The uses of this device are similar to those of the "fade." However, since it is a shorter process and interrupts the continuity of the film less, it is used more freely. Most commonly it is employed to represent the passage of time. Thus, a table set for dinner may dissolve into the same table after the depradations of the diners. In this manner a lapse of several hours is indicated.

In addition, the "dissolve" is often used to emphasize a similarity in form between two objects in succeeding shots. Since the two images literally appear to dissolve into one another, the device represents a species of growth or evolution wherein the first object changes into the second. In Chaplin's *The Gold Rush*, the following example of this occurs. A starving miner chases Charlie around a snow-bound shack with a view of satisfying his cannibalistic appetite. Charlie waves his arms frantically while trying to escape, and his gesticulating figure dissolves into a shot of a rooster with wings flapping. The clearly indicated similarity between the actor and the fowl makes the miner's illusion apparent.

c) The Wipe

The "wipe" is a process in which the image is apparently stripped from the screen as though peeled, to reveal another image underneath it. There are innumerable variations of this technique wherein the "peeling" seems to come from ten different directions simultaneously, or to be opening from the middle, etc. This device is limited in its expressive possibilities because it needlessly emphasizes the two dimensionality of the screen and thus interferes with the illusion.

The "fade," the "dissolve" and the "wipe" involve a lapse of time between shots and so disrupt the discontinuity upon which so much of filmic expression depends. With this in mind, it should be recognized that the cut is the proper filmic means of transition from shot to shot. These "alternatives to the cut" are employed only when some specific expressive purpose is served through their use.

—19

Part III—Sound

INTRODUCTION

The wails have died away. Sound, the monster that would destroy the "art of the film," has been reluctantly admitted to the bosom of the theorists. The introduction of sound caused justified consternation among those who had carefully fostered the silent medium, because it signalized an extended spree for the technicians. The film artists who had just begun to realize a proper and mature form for their medium, were roughly shouldered aside to make way for the officious sound engineers, the darlings of the new "talking machine."

The public clamored for sound movies, and the producers stumbled over each other in their haste to tap the new source of profits. In the great rush to re-equip dozens of studios and to produce sound movies, the form of the silent films which had been so painfully wrought was forgotten, and the first sound films represented art of as low a calibre as the early "photoplay."

At first, the microphone was a very recalcitrant instrument. It had to be placed "just so" in relation to he actors. Any movement of the camera involved expense and trouble because the sound set-up had to be correspondingly changed. In addition, recording was so imperfect that during the course of a dozen shots the same actor would be possessed of a dozen different voices. These conditions discouraged cutting, and the trend in the development of the film was reversed. The free discontinuity of the film, which had been so laboriously constructed, gave way to "100% real-life" reproductions of the drama.

It is characteristic of commercial enterprise that, in the rush to satisfy public demand, it should lose sight of theoretical considerations. Hollywood was no exception. Never a great respecter of "art" or the "kinema," the west coast studios proceeded to indiscriminately inject sound into the movies. The marvellous new sensation of sound, of "real sound," was exploited as an end in itself. Audiences doted on recordings of slamming doors, heavy breathing, clinking glasses, etc. Therefore, extraneous, meaningless sounds were interpolated into the film in a vain attempt to reproduce nature. The novelty wore off—but the habit persisted.

The American sudios were, of course, imitated by their foreign satellites. Even in Russia, where the silent film had truly evolved into an art form, the introduction of sound disrupted the entire procedure of film production. Only a few isolated directors recognized the proper function of sound, and proceeding to exploit it as a part of the whole, i.e., as a new creative element. Everyone else apparently "turned on the microphone" and started to make the film "naturalistic." "Naturalism" (as we trust we have proved) has no place in the film. So long as the film remains a medium for representation and not for reproduction, the "naturalistic" use of sound is not artistically acceptable, and it is no more reasonable to expect such a treatment of sound than it would be to ask for the naturalistic use of the visual element of the film.

In the silent film all impressions resulted from visual stimulation, i.e., from the graphic images which were projected on the screen. However, the sound film director has two stimulants with which to assail the senses of the audience. The projector now shares honors with the loud speaker. Both elements are powerful. Either one considered singly appears as a significant form of expression—sight (the silent film), and sound (the radio play)—and for this very reason their integration into a single medium is a delicate and dangerous process. Harnessed together, so that each draws a share of the load, the two may form a whirlwind team. But improperly exploited, so that one duplicates the efforts of the other, the combination will be as ineffectual as a team in which one member does the work. Worse still, the use of sound to echo visual effects is not only wasteful, but blunts the incisive expression which characterized the silent film.

The functions of sight and sound must be coordinated so that the full potentialties of both are realized. The two are so interwoven and so dependent upon each other for significance, that either of them considered alone would be meaningless. This is proper sound film. Conversely, in any film in which either sight or sound is the sole agency of expression, and the remaining element merely tautologous accompaniment, there has been an improper treatment of the medium, inevitably resulting in inferior expression. Examples of this latter type are often encountered in the stage plays which are "adapted" to the screen. The dialogue, which is the most important expressive factor of the drama, is retained, and, in addition, we are burdened with an elaborate filmic treatment of the same theme. In such cases, the images on the screen are merely accompaniment, add little to what the dialogue expresses, and serve no artistic purpose. This process, as well as that of adding sound to a visually conceived film, is an artistic heresy, analagous to adding color to a Rembrandt etching.

If it is appreciated that sound in the film must be treated exactly as any element in any art, i.e., as an aspect of nature which must be appropriately modified for expressive purposes, the ensuing discussion of the applications of sound will be more readily understood.

For purposes of exposition, we have divided sound into three categories. These are: 1) speech; 2) natural sound or noise; and)3 music.

I. THE COMMENTATIVE USE OF SOUND

This is a broad and inclusive category, easily the most comprehensive of the three which we shall discuss. The definition of "comment" indicates that it may be used in all of the following senses: observation, explanation, criticism, discussion and exposition.

a) Speech

We may again refer to the final sequence of *Janosik* for a satisfactory example of speech used for exposition. While the judge monotonously intones the words of the death sentence and the mode of execution, the camera carries us from face to face in the group. We see the assumed stolidity of the hero, the frustrate fury of the little boy who idolizes him, the blank expression of the soldiers and the weeping of the women. In this manner, the microphone and camera combine to enrich the content of the sequence. Repetition is avoided and the coordination of sight and sound becomes a cumulative process. This is in direct contradistinction to that procedure which would hold the face of the judge on the screen during the entire recital of the sentence. The latter treatment would be comparatively ineffectual because the visual element (the shot of the judge's face) would add little or nohing to the content of the sequence.

b) Natural Sound

It was mentioned before that the infinite world of incidental sounds is one which the director must carefully sift and filter. As always, he must include only such sounds as constructively add to the meaning.

In Chaplin's *Modern Times* there is a good example of incidental noise used commentatively. Our hero, imprisoned in an escape-proof feeding machine, is being fed an ear of corn which revolves automatically between his distended jaws. Something goes wrong with the machine, and the corn begins to revolve very rapidly. The kernels fly in all directions while the helpless Charlie goes through wild and futile contortions. The formerly gentle hum of the machine has by now grown into a veritable siren shriek which symbolizes the senseless mechanized retort to all of his excited gesticulations.

c) Music

In order to illustrate the commentative possibilities of music in the film let us adduce the following hypothetical example:

On the screen we visualize a large crowd massed about a platform on which a speaker is standing. The camera is at the outer fringe of the assemblage, so that while the speaker's gestures are visible, his facial expression is indistinct, and we cannot hear his speech. Yet it will appear that we can understand the sense of the speech through the commentative ability of the accompanying musical score. Wild music that grows soft would convey the impression that the orator was soothing the mob. Music of a reverse order would put inflammatory words in his mouth. A muted horn solo might suggest a eulogy. With an obvious theme like "Yes, We Have No Bananas," the speaker becomes a hypocrite deluding the crowd, and a brazen cacaphony would indicate that his words were drivel.

In this single example, then, we can appreciate the scope of music in an expository function.

II. CONTRASTIVE USE OF SOUND

Just as the director exploits the artistic device of contrast, both within the shot and in montage, so he may now avail himself of the contrast between the aural and visual elements of the medium.

a) Speech

An illuminating, if uninspired, example of the contrast of speech with the visual elements of the film may be remarked in the labor short, *Millions Of Us*, mentioned before. The protagonist, the same one who has gone to sleep hungry, wakes up in the full sunshine of a California day. It is apparently a holiday, and at a celebration in a park, a jowled, well-fed "type" is spouting platitudes on the glories of America, the opportunities for youth, etc. We hear his voice blaring through a public address system at the same time that we see the young bedraggled proletariat. The ironic climax is reached when the speaker emotionally describes the wealth of the land, the fruits of the soil and of the trees, "ours for the asking." As he says this, the hungry young man is standing before a fruit stand laden with the "choicest offerings of agriculture." He is prevented from picking up even a fallen apple by a righteously indignant guardian of the law.

b) Natural Sound

A similar contrast between poverty and affluence could have been achieved by coordinating a shot of the hungry fellow standing before a mansion with sounds of revelry from within.

c) Music

In the Russian film *Gypsies*, there is an excellent example of the use of contrastive music. The arrogant tribal chief is challenged to a duel by a poor commoner whom he has injured. The opponents retire to a wood where the fight with cruel knotted whips, the traditional dueling weapons, takes place. The camera is placed at the edge of the wood, where the anxious Gypsies wait for the winner. The only knowledge they have of the progress of the duel is the sound of the lashes. Finally, that ceases, and the suspense of the group increases until they see the bleeding chief, panting for breath, stagger out of the wood. Their first impression, that the leader has won, becomes confused when the other combatant, equally battered, follows him. The outcome of the fight is uncertain until the commoner, in a cracked and weary voice, breaks into a triumphal chant. The melody, contrasting with the bruised mouth from which it issues, emphasizes the exulting spirit of the victorious man.

III. EVOCATIVE USE OF SOUND

a) Speech

Primarily a theatrical device, the use of speech to evoke emotion is nevertheless serviceable in the film. However, this obvious application of sound is often overworked while the other expressive agencies of camera, montage and the sound track are neglected. Evocative speech is effectively employed in Alexander Korda's *Rembrandt*.

Charles Laughton, the Rembrandt of the film, returning to his father's home after years of absence, is seated at the humble dinner table. He reads the evening prayer to the devout family. The fluid Biblical poetry, read by a master of expression like Laughton, evokes a thrilling and solemn mood which impresses the spectator with the beauty of the faith of these unaffected Dutch country folk.

b) Natural Sound

An example of the proper use of "natural sound" for evocative purposes is the following. A man is nervously pacing the floor. The director wishes to indicate that the man's agitation is approaching hysteria. To accomplish this, the director may counterpoise against rapidly cut shots of nervous hands, twitching lips, moving figure, the steady metrical beat of the man's feet as he paces the floor. If the audience becomes party to his nervous tension, the steady "tom-tom" beat of his foot steps have succeeded in being more than just a corollary of the action.

c) Music

It is scarcely necessary to elaborate on the possibilities for the evocative uses of music. Music, whether in conjunction with the film or not, is a strongly evocative medium. A fine example of evocative music, properly coordinated with a film, is the closing sequence of *The Garden of Allah*.

Charles Boyer, a monk, "deserts" a Trappist monastery, and marries Marlene Dietrich. Despite their happiness, Boyer's conscience relentlessly denies him the full joy of freedom and love. When he is finally "discovered," the devout Marlene realizes that renunciation is their only salvation. When the final parting moment comes, the sun is shining as if in despite, contrasting the gorgeous spectrum of nature with the dull monotone of the cloister. If the director had not been able to evoke successfully a realization of the spiritual forces which can accomplish such a domination of will, the film must have ended falsely. Recognizing this, Boleslavski introduced a distinctive musical device; as Boyer's resolute figure diminished in size up the long monastery path, the audience heard the voices of a great choir increasing in volume. This great swelling hymn effectively symbolized the spiritual forces which had called forth their renunciation.

Suggested Reading

ARNHEIM, RUDOLF—*Film*. Published 1933 by Faber & Faber, London. Camera Manipulation and Discontinuity comprehensively discussed.

NICOLL, ALLARDYCE—*Film and Theatre*. Published 1936 by Thomas Y. Crowell, New York. An exposition of the "scope of the film." Distinguishes between stage and screen material.

PUDOVKIN—*Film Technique*. Published 1933 by George Newnes, London. A popularized discussion of film construction. Treatment is based on montage.

ROTHA, PAUL—*Celluloid, The Film Today*. Published 1931 by Longmans Green & Co., London. Good reviews of some of the best films.

SPOTTISWOODE, RAYMOND—*A Grammar of The Film*. Published 1935 by Faber & Faber, London. A carefully organized study of the applications of montage and sound.

PARNASSUS TO LET

PARNASSUS TO LET

An Essay about Rhythm in the Films

BY

ERIC WALTER WHITE

*Published by Leonard & Virginia Woolf at The
Hogarth Press, 52 Tavistock Square, London, W.C.1*
1928

Printed in Great Britain by
NEILL & Co., LTD., EDINBURGH.

"Come, Muse, placard 'Removed' and 'To Let' on the rocks of your snowy Parnassus."

WALT WHITMAN, *Song of the Exposition.*

PARNASSUS TO LET

ART-FORMS decay and are continually renewed.

The progress of science has a hand in this change.

The primitive epic, the *chanson de geste*, the ballad were all for recital. Literature was then a temporal art, just as music still is for the vast majority of people. But with the invention of printing by Gutenberg about 1450 the course of literature began to be changed. There was no longer any necessity for poems and chronicles to be read aloud. Those who wished to, and were rich enough, could possess them, printed, as a book, and read and reread them at their will. Literature began to lose its temporal quality. A man could get to know a poem or a story so well that he could review it in retrospect as a whole, just as if it were a painting, and he standing back at the correct distance; whereas, previously, only the first and last lines with a few striking passages in between had remained in his memory, standing out like peaks above the intervening valleys sunk in mist. With the bound book present on his shelf, as soon as one part of the story or poem became dim, he could easily revivify his memory by rereading that part and so restore the image. Much modern poetry that is thought to be difficult and obscure is so only because the sequence of ideas is no longer temporal; it is logical, but its point of departure and point of return are dictated by the artist's whim. The result is that at the first reading the poem is unintelligible, in fact it *cannot* be understood until the last line has been read, the complete circle described, and the poet's image re-created three-dimensionally in the reader's mind.

This change in the temporal quality of literature has altered the course of such art-forms as the epic, the *chanson de geste*, and the ballad. This is not to say that these art-forms are now never used. Mr Robert Graves has shown that it is still possible for the ballad to recur spontaneously in times of abnor-mality—but with a difference. Even *Paradise Lost* compared to the *Iliad* is like Liverpool Cathedral compared to Salisbury. The epic has passed by and crossed over towards the drama, as can be seen from Browning's *Ring and the Book* and Hardy's *Dynasts*.

But what new art-forms can we point to?

The novel and the cinema.

The novel is not much more than a

century and a half old, despite Apuleius, Lyly, and Addison. Of course, all modern histories of the novel start at least one or two thousand years ago and trace minutely throughout all literatures the indications of its coming birth. Unfortunately no one noticed these indications at the time; and it was not until the novel was an accomplished fact that the old pointers were discovered standing and (what is more) all pointing in the same direction.

The cinema is the newest of all the arts and has as yet barely come of age. Walt Whitman unconsciously was its prophet; and like the novel it has had its pointers too, but these are only just beginning to be discovered: in places Shakespeare's *Antony and Cleopatra* reads more like a film scenario than a drama, and what is Hogarth's *Marriage à la Mode* but the first six-reel comedy? Its birth was the fruit of an unnatural

12

attachment between the drama and painting, who called in science to act the midwife; and at times this offspring still betrays its bastard origin by making the mistake of imitating too closely either parent art. Most people will allow that the drama mothered the cinema; but such a paternity is certain to be called in question.

Since the time of Cimabue, painting has been freed from the necessity of being the handmaid successively of religion, history, morality (not to mention high-class pornography) and portraiture: this last by the scientific invention of photography in the last century. Without doubt painters will still continue to use all these as excuses to cover up the intolerable nudity of their æsthetic ideas. But to-day a young man wishing to have a likeness of himself finds a Cecil Beaton more reliable than a Picasso. In the photo-

13

grapher's studio he will be photographed in a sequence of different positions with all the usual accessories. Apart from the question of the photographer's imagination or a certain talent in the sitter, how far are we here from Charlie Chaplin in his one-man film, *One A.M.?* And, once Chaplin admitted, all the rest follows.

The cinema (for the good of its soul!) started out without textbooks telling it how it should go about to work; and what it has learnt during these first twenty years of its life, it has learnt by experience. The technique of scenario writing has been vastly improved, so much so in Chaplin's case that it has been improved away altogether, for his latest films have been directly created without written script. This is of importance, for it shows how completely the cinema has now succeeded in casting off the shackles of

14

literature, everywhere except in some European and American backwaters where old faults and prejudices still linger on. For too long literature poisoned the cinema by making her the most tempting offers of plots and titles —tempting, because the plots offered were ready-made and the titles of proved publicity value. Literature is one art, the cinema another: it was impossible that the cinema should continue to take orders from Lady Literature and live below stairs. And it is significant that out of the following random list of good films not one happens to be a screen adaptation of a novel or a play: *The Cruiser Potemkin*, *The Cabinet of Dr Caligari*, *The Woman of Paris*, *Warning Shadows*, *The Salvation Hunters*, *Vaudeville*, *The Pilgrim*, *Berlin*, and *The Marriage Circle*. In all these the cinema has found, more by intuition than by anything else, her true technique.

15

Apart from the superficial attractions of literature, the cinema (as its origin made inevitable) has had to learn how to escape from the danger of dramatic scenes and pictorial shots. For many years intelligent appreciation of films was held up by the appalling stupidity of scenes, which may once have been dramatic on the stage, but which had been so literally translated into the cinema that they became deserts of monotony wherein long close-ups of the emotional heroine were divided from long close-ups of the passionate hero by wads of subtitles that were supposed to make articulate the incessant lip-service of the two stars. Producers have at last learnt the danger of retarding the visual action by subtitle after subtitle, and have even found it possible, as in the case of *Warning Shadows*, to produce quite intelligible films without any subtitles at all. Except in the case of

16

comedies where a good joke is never amiss, it is safe to say that, the fewer and shorter the subtitles, the more chance for the film itself.

Similar, but not so obvious, is the danger of the pictorial shot. The most essential quality of the cinema being motion, it stands to reason that any pictorial shot is apt to make a film static and to sap its dynamic force. Sometimes this is harmless. A still photograph of a landscape may act as an excellent jumping-off place at the beginning of a film, before the action has had time to gather way. A similar still is useful at the end, to bring the audience's feelings back to the normal plane. Three stills of three different stone lions, shown in rapid succession at the beginning of the bombardment of Odessa in *The Cruiser Potemkin,* gave the same plastic and rousing effect as three notes blown on a trumpet. One

of the most notable moments in *Berlin*
was when the rhythmic acceleration,
emotional tension, and musical climax
of the arrival by train were suddenly
succeeded by quiet photographic stills:
of the city, lifeless as a picture post-
card in the dawn, of the smokeless
factories, of the deserted streets: each
accompanied by a low chord *pianissimo*.
Still followed after still, like so many
lantern slides, until down an exhausted
street came the first wind of the day,
blowing a piece of white paper along
the dry pavement, over and over. As
for pictorial shots, one of a prison scene
in the prologue to *Vaudeville* was
obviously based on a well-known painting of Van Gogh's *La Ronde des Prison-
niers*, which (it seems not to be so well
known) Van Gogh painted after Doré.
But the mere fact that the prisoners
were in motion was sufficient to pre-
serve the prologue from any ill effect

that an absolutely static shot might
have had on it. On the other hand,
there was a scene in *The Woman of Paris*,
where a mother was bowed in grief over
the bier of her son, which, although not
directly reminiscent of any known painting, was definitely pictorial in quality,
and left an unpleasant feeling in the
audience's mind, partly of false emphasis
and partly of sentimentality.

These few examples are sufficient to
show that the cinema has gained its
experience in a hard field, threatened
by false bogeys, hindered by the absence
of tradition. Before it can go forward
with fresh strength and more directness
of purpose, the ground it has covered
must be critically examined and the
foundations of a true tradition laid.
The time for that has now come. But
although during the last few years the
cinema has drawn forth a host of
ephemeral literature (most of it French),

none of it seems to give serious consideration to what (at least to judge by the other arts) ought to be a most important element in any film—namely, Rhythm. Film-producers themselves naturally have little spare time or inclination to experiment—their job is too risky for that. And so it is that the knowledge of rhythm in the cinema remains extremely vague. For though a certain amount may be gathered from analogy with the other arts, yet in the end the true laws and manifestations of rhythm in the cinema will have to be found out by trial and experiment in that medium alone.

What follows in this essay is a loose and all too inadequate attempt towards a synthesis. Any analogy shall be drawn mainly from English poetry where the workings of rhythm can most easily be followed: analogies drawn from painting or from music (however modern) are liable to prove deceptive.

Gerard Manley Hopkins, to whom the debt of the Sitwells, Miss Stein, and even James Joyce is obvious but as yet unacknowledged, wrote in 1883 (two years before Stevenson's pleasant but too curious essay on the technical elements of style in literature) a preface to his unpublished poems, wherein we find the following passage concerning the rhythm of the English five-foot verse:— "If, however, the reversal (trochee for iamb) is repeated in two feet running, especially so as to include the sensitive second foot, it must be due either to great want of ear or else is a calculated effect, the superinducing or *mounting* of a new rhythm upon the old; and since the new or mounted rhythm is actually heard and at the same time the mind naturally supplies the natural or standard foregoing rhythm, for we do not forget what the rhythm is that by rights we should be hearing, two rhythms are in some manner running at once and we have something answerable to counterpoint in music, which is two or more strains of tune going on together, and this is Counterpoint Rhythm." This passage is most interesting and enlightening, especially for its inaccuracies. The musical analogy is inexact, probably owing to some confusion in Hopkins's mind over the exact meaning of tune. One is left with the suspicion that he did not realise that a single unaccompanied tune can have rhythm (just as well as a passage in intricate counterpoint), so long as the single tune in itself implies a metre. It is because Hopkins ignores metre that he is led into the difficulty of making unnecessary distinctions between two or three different rhythms, whereas what he calls natural or standard rhythm is really metre, and his counterpoint rhythm, rhythm itself. With these substitutions the passage becomes quite comprehensible. It seems that wherever we find rhythm there must be, underlying, some simple metre. In French verse this metre may be numerical, a fixed number of syllables to each line; in English accentual, as in the following scheme, ˘ -|˘ -|˘ -|˘ -|˘ -; in music a common metre is made up by four regularly recurring accents of the following roughly proportional intensities: 4 2 3 1. Consequently, in examining rhythm in the cinema we must look for what can be used as an underlying metre. The metre found may not be strictly adhered to; but, as always, exceptions will only help to prove the rule. To begin with, a certain number of examples will be collected, wherein several films have appeared to possess obvious, pleasing, and successful rhythms.

An excellent example of simple episodic rhythm, remarked by most people, occurred in Chaplin's great film, *The Woman of Paris*. There the arrival of a train in a provincial station was indicated by a gradually slowing succession of lighted oblongs thrown across the station wall from the carriage windows. Simultaneously with this motor pattern the woman (who was standing on the platform) moved her face across in the same direction, but very much more slowly, as she watched the arrival of this train that was to take her to Paris. A local metre had been set up, regular visually, geometrically progressive temporally; and above that, a simple movement, sufficient to make the whole scene absolutely thrilling.

An intelligent experiment in the rousing of emotion by rhythmic acceleration was made in the first edition of an English film, *The Little People*. The first shots of the film showed the slow beating of a drum to attract people to the performance of a marionette show. One saw people hear the drum and start swaying their heads in time with it. Then, as the speed of the beating increased, one saw the villagers going to the show, walking at first, then running, children tripping up in their hurry, and finally the audience clapping rapidly. Following three isolated drum taps, the curtain rose and the show began. How successful this his opening scene would have been with the public cannot be said, as the film was only released in a most unfortunately mutilated condition.

But it is doubtful whether any film before *The Salvation Hunters* showed a conscious effort made to set up a continuous rhythmic feeling; and there it only persisted strongly through the

25

first half of the film, the scene of which was laid on a mud-dredger. This dredger worked continuously, either the claw-bucket travelling up and down dribbling filth, or the crane-neck swinging out over the mud-barge and back. This was movement in three dimensions of a slow but regular kind, and it proved to be soothing and not distracting. Other shots had the usual fixed backgrounds of walls, doors, etc. And these two series of scenes were alternated in certain simple ratios, according to the demands of the action as it moved through one scene to another. Here, at first, it is difficult to say whether we have an example of simple or counterpoint rhythm in its truest sense: whether the regularly recurring movements of the dredger, or the simple permutations and combinations of the scenes with moving and fixed backgrounds, provide the metre.

26

This film, made at a negligible cost
by an enterprising group of Hollywood
unemployed, came in for some curious
treatment at the hands of the critics.
Iris Barry in her disappointing book,
Let's Go to the Pictures, speaks of it as
follows:—"Chaplin, one heard, hailed
the picture as a masterpiece. When
Chaplin opens his mouth, all the critics
yap in unison. *The Salvation Hunters*
was acclaimed throughout the world.
It was a dismal failure. When it had
gone its rounds, Chaplin said that he
had thought he would see whether the
cinema audiences had any sense. He
thought he would praise a bad picture
and see how many would swallow what
he said." This little trick of Chaplin's
lacks confirmation: let it suffice to
point out that on the strength of this
picture alone he took Georgia Hale and
starred her in *The Gold Rush* in the
place of Lita Grey. Iris Barry was not

the only critic who misunderstood the importance of *The Salvation Hunters*. Other critics made the same mistake, probably because they were unused to any sensible handling of rhythm in films, and distrusted the term itself on account of its misuse by directors of the so-called absolute or abstract films that hail from Paris.

The average Englishman is so afraid of having his leg pulled by Jean Cocteau or any of Cocteau's friends to-day, that he is apt to lose his temper instead of laughing. Just as Comte Etienne de Beaumont's drawing-room ballet, *Mercure*, as irresponsible as a charade, annoyed the London critics when Diaghilev put it on in the summer of 1927, so the Comte's abstract film, entitled *A Quoi Rêvent les Jeunes Films?* puzzled and upset the cinema critics in 1925. The truth is that the film proved to be faintly amusing but plotless. There

28

was no interest to link together the jumble of haphazard photographs, many of which had obviously been based on the studies of Man Ray. *Entr'acte* was a little better because it contained at least the shadow of an idea, scenes of an eccentric funeral being shown alternately in quick and slow motion. Then came the *Ballet Mécanique* of Fernand Léger, George Antheil, and Dudley Murphy, of which the French critic, Monsieur Charensol, has spoken as follows:—"Usually in every film there are two absolutely distinct elements, the subject and its realisation: the first appealing to the intellect and the second to the visual sense. But in the *Ballet Mécanique* the authors have entirely done away with the subject, leaving the spectator free to concentrate on the visual realisation. This is composed of a succession of pictures: animate and inanimate objects, machines,

29

tools, and geometric forms, following each other in obedience to a preconceived rhythm." Nothing could be clearer or more preposterous. Probably the best of all these films has been Man Ray's own *Emak Bakia*, the Basque title of which emphasises its lack of pretentiousness. This film did not aim at being a complete work of art; it was content to offer itself merely as a sequence of extracts from a sensitive artist's notebook. And that is really what all the other abstract films are— just a collection of rough jottings and fragments, valuable only in so much as they have improved somewhat the range and standard of a photography whose only previous licence had been to photograph all its fluffy heroines *flou* at sentimental moments, and have given directors a clue for such abstract aberrations as might be dictated by the subject of their films—for example, the dream in *The Nibelungs*, the acrobatic and the fair scenes in *Vaudeville*, the machinery in *Berlin* and *Metropolis* —and for such superimpositions as may be found in the German World War films and Gance's *Napoleon*, or such virtual superimpositions as the stock exchange, factory, and war scenes in Pudowkin's *End of St Petersburg*, which are alternated so quickly that the eye can no longer distinguish between them and take them in separately.

It is not the abstract film, but the right use of the abstract shot, that is important in so far as cinematic rhythm is concerned, because the abstract shot provides an easy and obvious way of obtaining contrast and emphasis. That its full possibilities have not yet been exploited can be seen in quite minor films, such as Monte Blue's *Wolf's Clothing*, where an enterprising producer suddenly provided an excellently

31

rhythmic scene on a New York subway where a train had got out of control, and also some very creditable attempts to portray the awakening feelings of a drunk man: distorting lenses being used on the people he saw, the furniture magnified to three or four times its usual size, and the actions of the bewildered man slightly slow-motioned.

The conclusion arrived at after the examination of abstract films, that it is not the abstract *film* but the abstract *shot* that is likely to prove of importance where cinematic rhythm is concerned, provides a clue that may be well worth following up. What is a shot? A shot is any length of film taken by the camera without break, and occupies normally the same time on the screen as in reality. As soon as the camera man ceases to turn the handle, the shot ends, even though the same scene, the same characters, may be used for the next shot. Although the shots are continuous on the screen (except where divided by subtitles, during which the rhythm of the film, and the acceptance of that rhythm by the audience, remains in suspense), yet the passage from one shot to another usually indicates a little temporal gap or mental comma; and may be said to act as a cæsura. Naturally, care is taken during the cutting of a film to run the shots together in such a sequence that the minimum of discomfort is experienced by the eye in jumping from one to another. The travelling camera has sometimes been used to try to smudge out these cæsuras. But the result is, that though the main parts of the shots have a fixed focus, the same as before, they are linked by a kind of no-man's-land, of little importance in itself, because during the time that the camera shifts

its focus and imitates the mannerisms
of the human eye it is practically impossible for any new movement of
importance to be initiated. On
occasions this can be quite effective,
although its use needs to be much more
restrained than it was in *The Rat*.
Nevertheless, it may be truly said that
these cæsuras punctuate a film. We
shall see from *Vaudeville* how important
it is that they should arrive at the just
moment, not a fraction of a second
late; and in *The Salvation Hunters* we
have already found it necessary that
where they divide two sets of scenes of
different characteristics they should
occur at intervals determined by suit-
ably simple ratios.[1] Then, may it not

[1] Monsieur Moussinac in his well-meaning but
inadequate book, *La Naissance du Cinéma*, has
some complicated diagrams showing several of the
simplest ratios in which shots from two or three
different sets of scenes may be combined. It

be that the basis of cinematic metre is cæsural and not accentual? that rhythm is built up by motion and emotion deployed from shot to shot? whether in a continuous pattern, or a richer and more complicated woof wherein a certain thread of motion or emotion, instead of being developed straight forward, is dropped out of the pattern for a time, only to be taken up again later and the loose thread drawn on right across the intervening warp?

It may be objected that a film has its accents just as much as a piece of music; that since a film makes its appeal to an audience through the particular to the

would be much more to the point if Lotte Reiniger could be persuaded to publish her diagrams and calculations relating to the fight of the sorcerer and the witch, and the synchronisation of the ringing of the bells and the tune of the flute-player with Zeller's music, in her silhouette film *Achmet*.

general, so an accent is bound to occur
as each particular point is made. This
is true. A film certainly has its stresses,
which may be caused in various ways:
decrease of focal distance, lengthening
of time value, any significant motion
on the part of the actors. But these
stresses are irregular in occurrence and
always go to build up, or drop away
from, one of the climaxes in a film.
Their growth arises out of the inner
necessity of the subject, and so they
cannot correspond to the regular accent
that is the fundamental of musical
metre. For, in any work of art, metre
is a foundation which must be clearly
established, or at least suggested; once
set going it persists mechanically.
Rhythm is superimposed and is organic.
Rhythm and metre may be said to set
each other off like colours shot. In a
film it is the cæsura alone whose
recurrence is frequent and regular

enough to warrant its use as the basis of cinematic metre.

Rhythm appears to be most obviously successful in a film when motional and emotional rhythms alternate, and the appeal to the spectator is at once visual and mental, there being no question of doing away with the subject nor of leaving anyone free to concentrate on the visual realisation alone, since that, rather than emphasise rhythm, would destroy it altogether.

The device where part of the action passes on a moving vehicle, whether car, tram, bus, or train, has (of course) been a favourite one with the producers of comedies ever since the earliest days of the cinema. But its possibilities can best be seen in such intelligently made films as Buster Keaton's *General*, Harold Lloyd's *For Heaven's Sake*, and Charlie Chaplin's infinitely more subtle *Pay Day*, where a service of midnight buses, which poor Charlie seems fated not to catch, act as metronomes and imprint their peculiar rhythm on the close of the film. Such motional scenes must be made with great restraint if they are to prove successful. Although movement is the breath of life to the cinema, yet it is of no use to photograph movement and nothing but movement. Without continued reference to the norm anything extraordinary eventually becomes meaningless and commonplace. Movement loses its effect if it is not contrasted with the firm and well-set earth. That is why, when Harold Lloyd gets on a bus with a handful of drunk men, it is necessary for the camera to pretend not only that it too is on the bus in order to photograph their antics at close quarters, but also that it is a common pedestrian on the sidewalk who sees this strangely driven vehicle come careering down the street towards him. Similarly, in *Vaudeville*, the audience in the Winter Garden sees the acrobats swinging like little white pendulums high up in the roof of the hall; and the acrobats see the audience, walls, lights in the ceiling, walls, audience far below them, walls, lights in the ceiling, in one continuous flux and reflux. Giddiness.

It is not so easy to give examples of how emotion may be deployed from shot to shot. To take a simple case: when in the Ufa production of *Cinderella* the sister cut her foot in order to fit it to the shoe, the succeeding scenes where she appears, pale and suffering, in her bridal robes and leaning on her mother's arm, would have lacked their tense rhythm, had not the audience known that every movement she made must have been agony, and that she was only supported by her mother's determination. Better still, the opening of Chaplin's *Pilgrim*:—First shot:

39

A warder comes out of a prison-gate and pastes a notice on the wall. A close-up of the notice reveals information about an escaped convict and a photo of Charlie. Second shot: A bather returns to find his clothes gone and a convict's uniform left in their place. Third shot: A curate walking up a station platform. A gust of wind blows off his hat. He retrieves it and turns round. It is Charlie. Three strands making a single knot.

If cinematic metre is cæsural, it follows that it is of the greatest importance that the cæsuras should occur at the correct moments in a film; that is to say, that the shots should be of the right length, neither too long nor too short, and that they should be combined with each other in the best order. When this has been well done by a film-editor, the result ought to be perfectly balanced and satisfying. But who is to say whether the censors and exhibitors of the world will allow such a film to be shown in its perfect mint form? As is well known, each country, each town, has its board of censors: the result is that Russian films are almost taboo in Western Europe, the true *Metropolis* may not be shown in England, nor the true *Vaudeville* in Birmingham, and even Chaplin (on the merest whisper of "divorce") is liable to be banned in Chicago and the United States. *Metropolis* as seen in England was quite different from the original film: thrills were deleted, a dance scene banned, the whole moral of the story altered: consequently the acting became illogical, the psychology false, and the balance and rhythm of the original film completely wrecked. Yet *Dawn*, though banned by Sir Austen Chamberlain in England, was shown wherever the local authorities chose to license it.

41

This is a disgraceful state of affairs.
The cinema, unlike literature, is an
immediately international art. It is
already much more international than
music or painting can hope to become
for many years, despite cheap colour-
printing and the radio. Not only does
a film ignore frontiers like an aeroplane,
but it comes nearer the heart of mankind than any of the other arts. If the
muses may be suspected of political
tendencies, the deity that presides over
the cinema is certainly Socialist. As
Walt Whitman cried when he had
succeeded in enticing the Muse over
from empty Parnassus to the New York
Exposition, "She's here, installed amid
the kitchen ware!"—he might have
added prophetically, "the Cinderella
of the arts." Although so young, the
cinema has proved its worth, to judge
from the influence it has already exerted
on the other arts. What modern ballet

owes it can be seen from *La Pastorale* and the slow-motion scenes in *The Blue Train* and *Apollo Musagetes*. Even James Joyce in *Tristan and Isolda* seems to be emulating the universality of the cinema in his attempt to break down the barriers of language by using words or word-fractions taken indiscriminately from about a dozen different tongues. And the works of Cendrars and Ramuz are widely known. The cinema is too old still to be treated as a naughty child. And yet the censor seems to find it necessary to mutilate masterpieces like *Vaudeville* and *Metropolis* (and, for that matter, Chaplin's *Woman of Paris*) before they can be shown in this country.

Could we not take a salutary lesson from Germany? There *The Cruiser Potemkin* was first shown with cuts, most of these coming in the famous Odessa Steps' scene. Naturally Meisel's music had to be similarly

43

mutilated to match. But when early in 1928 the censor licensed the whole of Eisenstein's later, but less successful, film, *October*, or *Ten Days that Shook the World*, there remained no adequate reason why the *Potemkin* should still be banned. With considerable wisdom the censor rescinded his decree and at last allowed this masterpiece to be shown in its entirety. Only then could the full effect of the Steps' scene be judged, one of the most perfect rhythmic episodes in any film. Given the visual metre of the long glissando of the steps, descending terrace by terrace, Eisenstein superimposed on it four different movements: (1) The regular descent of the firing-line, step by step, step by step—*Fire!* (This movement emphasised strongly the metre of the steps.) (2) The panic of the crowd flying helter-skelter, those shot falling dead, those wounded trying to crawl into safety. (3) The contrary motion of the mother, who, finding her son shot dead by her side, picked up his body and returned with it to defy the firing-line. (4) The young widow, who, being shot, fell against her baby's perambulator so that it began to bump down the steps: bump, bump, bump—a short landing— and then, bump, bump, bump, bump, again. This movement was the most surprising of all, because the most incongruous; yet it, together with a great part of (3), had been entirely cut away from the first version. As shown in Berlin in 1928, this scene was perfect with the tragic perfection of the opening movement of Beethoven's Last Symphony ; whereas such deliberately thought-out rhythmic constructions as Lotte Reiniger's silhouette films, *Achmet* and *Cinderella*, can never achieve more than the delicate perfection of Cimarosa.

45

Then, let what cutting has to be done
be done at the time that a film is edited;
for it is almost entirely to the editor of a
film that its ultimate rhythm is due, and
any later alteration of his work will only
upset the balance of the whole. How
much depends on careful editing can be
seen from a comparison of *Vaudeville*
with Chaplin's *Gold Rush*. It is one of
the signs of Chaplin's genius that he
never holds a scene too long. In *The
Gold Rush* there is a moment when
Charlie prepares a New Year's Eve
party, the guests do not turn up, and
the whole film is on the point of sliding
into the most embarrassing sentimentality. A moment longer and the thing
were done. But that moment never
comes. Just on the right side of time
Chaplin switches off and executes the
miraculous Oceana Roll. The situation is saved by one of the most brilliant
moments in the whole history of the

46

cinema. In *Vaudeville*, however, the tempo of the film is deliberately slowed up in order to give the murder scene a ponderous impressivity. But it is undoubtedly slowed up just a fraction too much. The impassivity of Emil Jannings ceases to awe one and begins to become slightly ludicrous—a dangerous thing to happen at the climax of any film. Had the editor cut two or three seconds, no more, off the length of most of the shots, that mistake would have been avoided (although it is always possible that those few seconds represent just the difference between the Teutonic and the British temperaments).

But, the point to be emphasised is this, that cutting is primarily the duty of the film editor, and not of any haphazard board of censors. Any later interference with a film is bound to upset the continuity of both its metre and rhythm, to react unfavourably on the

47

minds and nervous systems of the audience, and to give as unsatisfactory results as a performance of Beethoven's *Eroica* with the "false horn entry" removed, or an exhibition of Raphael's *Transfiguration* with the figure of the epileptic boy and his outstretched arms cut out. Perhaps a solution of these difficulties would be for the League of Nations to set up an international board of censors that should pass all films or cause them to be modified, once and for all. But that, no doubt, is too simple an ideal for these hard times.

OXFORD—CLIFTON—POTSDAM.

PRINTED IN GREAT BRITAIN BY NEILL AND CO., LTD. EDINBURGH.